Cafés and Comets After Midnight
and Other Poems

NIKOS ENGONOPOULOS

Cafés and Comets After Midnight
and Other Poems

Translated by
David Connolly

AIORA

David Connolly is retired Professor of Translation Studies at the Aristotle University of Thessaloniki. He has translated over forty books with works by contemporary Greek writers. His translations have received awards in the USA, the UK and Greece.

© Errietti Engonopoulou
© for this edition: Aiora Press 2020

First edition April 2020

All rights reserved. No part of this publication may be reproduced, stored in a retrieval system, or transmitted, in any form or by any means, electronic, mechanical, photocopying, recording or otherwise, without written permission of the publishers.

ISBN: 978-618-5369-14-9

AIORA PRESS
11 Mavromichali st.
Athens 10679 - Greece
tel: +30 210 3839000
www.aiorabooks.com

for Errietti
pillar-box red...
D. C.

Contents

Introduction 11

Poems

From: DO NOT DISTRACT THE DRIVER
    Polyxeni 23
    Amazons 25
    Perhaps 27
    The airport's wooden idols 29

From: THE CLAVICEMBALOS OF SILENCE
    A flute in the hecatomb yard 31
    Parapluies 33
    On the mountains of Myoupolis I 39
                         II 41
                         III 47
    Consequence 49
    Morning song 55

From: THE RETURN OF THE BIRDS
    A soldier's song 61
    Love's snare 71
    Love's seventh song 75
    The last appearance of Judas Iscariot ... 79
    "Souvenir of Constantinople" 81

  Stateless forcibly deported 85
From: ELEUSIS
  Cafés and comets after midnight 89
From: IN THE FLOURISHING GREEK TONGUE
  Lady Celeste 93
  Orpheus Xenophobe 95
From: IN THE VALE OF ROSERIES
  Poem-imitation of numerous hymns
    suitable for an all-male choir to ecclesiastical
    music by Johann Sebastian Bach 97
  The icon 105
  On the holy Jews 107
  The cricket 111
  Concerning hamadryads 117
  The poem of Esther Bessalel 119
  The surprise 125

Chronology 127

Book-length English Translations 133

Index of Greek Titles 135

Introduction

> *I never went over to surrealism.*
> *I always had surrealism inside me...*
>
> Nikos Engonopoulos

Engonopoulos' recognition today as a major Greek poet would have been impossible to imagine given the outcry following the publication of his first collection. Of all the Greek surrealist poets, he was the most provocative and uncompromising and has rightly been referred to as its enfant terrible. His first public association with the surrealist movement in Greece came with the publication in February 1938 of his translations of poems by Breton, Éluard and other French surrealist poets in a collective volume entitled *Surrealism I*. In March of the same year, his first poems appear in the literary magazine *O Kyklos* followed in June by the publication of his first collection, *Do Not Distract The Driver*. The hostility on the part of both the press and critics was unprecedented in Greek literary history. In the notes that he appended to the re-publication of his first two collections some thirty years later, Engonopoulos recalls: "We had already had intimations of what was to come with the publication of the magazine. When the book appeared, however, the 'scandal' that was caused not only exceeded anything that had ever before been seen in Greek letters, but went beyond the bounds of the wildest imagination. [...] Magazines, newspapers, *le premier chien coiffé venu*, parodied and derisively quoted my poems." But the "scandal" provoked by his first collection was not sufficient to deter the poet and, in September of the following year (1939), he published his second collection *The Clavicembalos of Silence*, which was received in similar fashion by the "intellectual" circles in Athens given its subversive and equally revolutionary poetry.

If Engonopoulos' poetry and the poetry of other Greek surrealist poets subsequently gained recognition and proved fruitful in Greece, this was because both he and his fellow Greek poets adapted the surrealism of Breton and the French poets to the Greek reality. What we find in the work of these poets are not the complexes of the subconscious but the ecstasy. Greek surrealist poetry, in general, is characterized by what one of its exponents, Nanos Valaoritis, refers to as *"hellenomageia"* (Greek enchantment), consisting of things sensuous, intoxicating, legendary, commonplace, of flowers, birds, insects, angels, perfumes, place names, mythological heroes, of light and sun — a particularly Greek reality, where, it might be added, the irrationality inherent in surrealism is more a way of life than a neurosis. Breton is reported to have once said: "We don't have to import Surrealism into Greece. The land itself is surrealistic". And according to Nobel Laureate, Odysseus Elytis, also influenced in his early work by surrealism, it was precisely this anti-rationalistic aspect of surrealism that appealed to the Greek poets. He explains that surrealism contained a supernatural element that enabled them to form a kind of alphabet out of purely Greek elements with which to express themselves.

This is certainly true in Engonopoulos's case. He created his own unique and personal idiom (unlike anything else in Greek letters) through which he converses with the Greek tradition using the tenets of surrealism. Speaking in 1954, he says: "Personally, I don't believe in surrealism as a school. Yet it suits me. What I tried to do was to renew it with Greek elements. To add to it Greek metaphysics, to elevate it beyond a simple mannerism, which is where it stops abroad". The elements he uses to create his poetic alphabet belong, thematically and linguistically, to the historical Greek consciousness even if they are filtered through his own highly idiosyncratic and personal consciousness. In the same way, many poems of purely personal fantasy are interspersed with overt or covert references to all historical phases of the Greek tradition.

Yet his ability to reshape and transform is not limited to the elements of tradition. He has the ability, common to great artists and poets, to create myth out of the mundane and insignificant. His mythopoeia enables him to reveal in the most commonplace and disparate objects and events in everyday life and in the simplest coincidences, combinations that are magic and unique, that without any longer having a connection with reality (that are *irrational*), nevertheless come to constitute a new reality of their own.

In many ways, Engonopoulos is the most orthodox surrealist of his generation, as one might expect from someone who said of himself: "I never went over to surrealism, I always had surrealism inside me". Yet, as one perspicacious critic and contemporary poet has pointed out, surrealism fits him like an "uncomfortable corset". The difference between his poetry and painting and that of the orthodox French and other Surrealists is that whereas they used irrationality to sever the bonds with tradition, he used it as a "connecting link", as a means of inventing a convincing continuity that would revitalize and unite the scattered fragments of a distant cultural past. And this is perhaps the source of the intellectual strain noted by many in his work. For, although his poetic images clearly well up out of the subconscious, it is equally clear, as translator and critic Kimon Friar remarks, that "they flow into the control of a highly conscious will".

If it was Engonopoulos's irreverent and subversive use of Greek tradition, of the historical rather than the individual consciousness, that upset the critics, it was also his provocative and subversive use of the Greek language. In this, he was not unique among Greek surrealist poets. One of the first reactions to the tenets of surrealism on the part of Greek poets is connected with the use of both katharevousa, the purist language, and demotic, the colloquial and popular language, which constituted the peculiarly Greek diglossia. It should be noted, however, that the Greek surrealist poets did not simply make use of this diglossia by mixing elements of katharevousa and demotic, but challenged the conventions of diglossia by flagrantly violating them. By juxtaposing linguistic styles conventionally seen as separate, they challenged all artificial and rational constraints on the free operation of the unconscious. In other words, in poetry which is characterized by automatic writing, or which flows unchecked (to whatever degree) from the subconscious, it would be unreasonable to exclude katharevousa as being a part of the Greek consciousness and, most likely, of the Greek subconscious. Just as Greek surrealism gave the same weight to the logical and the absurd, the significant and the insignificant, it could not ignore either demotic or katharevousa, or any other historical phases of the Greek language for that matter.

What characterizes Engonopoulos's poetic diction, however, is not just the use of katharevousa but the creative juxtaposition of disparate and often conflicting linguistic elements (as with the content of his poetry, so also with the diction). His idiosyncratic language is astonishingly diverse and colourful, deceptively simple yet composite. It does not only alternate between demotic and katharevousa, but draws on the byzantine and post-byzantine period and is embellished with dialectical and sociolectical forms and with loan words and foreign words (Turkish, Albanian, French, Italian, Latin), often within the same poem. The way that he combines heterogeneous linguistic elements in the text recalls the technique that we recognize in his paintings. He applies layers of language to his text just as he does layers of paint to his canvas. As a poetic technique it focuses the attention of the reader on the linguistic medium itself.

Engonopoulos himself has on more than one occasion explained that his "mixed" language is the language he speaks and that the only legitimate language for poets is the Greek language in all its aspects. Again in the appended "Notes" to the republication of his first two collections, he says: "I will confine myself to just a few lines about the language I use, and which has often been characterized, in the form of a reproach, as being "mixed". I have to say that, very simply, this is the language I speak. And besides, is not the prime importance to be understood by those who really do wish to understand? The legitimate language, for us, is the Greek language. Those fanatic views concerning a "mixed", "purist" or "popular" language have absolutely no meaning whatsoever. [...] I came to realize that there is only one Greek language. And that it is more a lack of prudence that leads one to stubbornly become devoted to one single form of it, to scorn that unimaginable wealth, that horde of treasure at one's disposal, instead of drawing on it freely, with respect and care of course, so as to adorn one's verse and reinforce one's meaning." And elsewhere, he states: "The Greek language is one. It would be foolish not to avail ourselves of this, to disregard its enormous treasures, all its forms: ancient, antiquated, contemporary, popular and dialectical…".

Engonopoulos may have claimed to have always had surrealism inside him, but his work goes beyond surrealism. Over and above its surrealist elements, what distinguishes his poetry is a dramatic dimension that puts the — by definition — optimistic vision of surrealism on a more human level. His poems and paintings are all dramatically "staged" down to the minutest detail. One always has the feeling that everything is premeditated in terms of the result and the impression that it is intended to have on the reader or viewer. His poems and paintings often serve as a stage for the absurd, for dream and also for nightmare. On this stage, whether on canvass or the page, move faceless bodies or bodies with masks for faces. Phantoms from the Greek past, alienated contemporary man, personas of the poet. It is not without significance that, throughout his life, not least for financial reasons, Engonopoulos designed stage sets and costumes for the theatre.

This ever-present dramatic aspect in his work is, however, often tempered and, indeed, subverted by his wry, sardonic humour. Of course, humour is also one of the most effective ways of achieving the stated surrealist aim to create a rupture with convention. It shakes established views, challenges custom, undermines convention, but also (and this is the main aim of art for Engonopoulos) it is a source of consolation and encouragement for both the poet and reader.

Another constant feature of his poetry which, like humour, tempers the dramatic aspect is the underlying sensuality and eroticism found throughout his poetry and which is comparable to that found in Cavafy. Many poems and paintings take their themes from famous couples from mythology with the prime example being Orpheus and Eurydice. Mythical, symbolic and actual (being part of his personal mythology), countless female figures parade through his poetry: Eurydice, Euterpe, Eleonora, Polyxeni, Pulcheria, Maria, Laura, Katerina, Esther, Adelaïs, heroic maidens, virgins sometimes white and slender, sometimes cruel and loveless, beautiful Creoles, naked women and saintly women, his future wife, Eleni; all of them mysterious and enigmatic, sensuous and erotic, inspiring and comforting, donators of longing and serenity. The theme of poet and muse, so prevalent in his painting, is equally prevalent, but in various guises, in his poetry. These muses elevate the poet and are elevated by the poet. But in Engonopoulos's work, the female figure is something more too. She becomes the symbol of a restless, exciting and often scandalous eroticism that functions in keeping with basic surrealist aims to rupture social conventions and accepted notions of propriety.

Engonopoulos was awarded the National Prize for Poetry in 1958 for his collection, *In the Flourishing Greek Tongue*, which suggests the hostility toward his work had finally abated and he had at last achieved recognition as an established poet. Another twenty years would pass between his receiving this award and the publication of his next collection, *In the Vale of Roseries*, in 1978, for which he again received the National Prize for Poetry. It is, perhaps, questionable whether one should read anything into this long period of silence, though some critics attribute it to his dedication to painting and his other professional obligations.

It is true that Engonopoulos had always made it clear that he considered himself first a painter and afterwards a poet, and nowhere more so than in the notes he wrote to accompany the poems he published in *In the Vale of Roseries*. Here, he expressly states: "I was never a systematic writer or systematic littérateur. The one great love of my life was painting. Whatever time I do not devote to painting is, in my view, time wasted. But of course a painting does not constantly demand the total dedication of mind and heart. There are moments, I could say, when the hand moves by itself. Yet the mind is always working. It's then that I avail myself and reflect on numerous things, or, more commonly, I make up songs. After work, if I commit these songs to paper, all well and good, otherwise I simply forget them". However, and despite what he says himself, he is certainly more than just a painter who wrote poems in his spare time and I think there is more of an integral connection between his poems and paintings than is often imagined, as one might expect when both works came from the same artistic inspiration and sensibility. One has the impression, comparing these works, that the poems are often commentaries on the paintings and the paintings visual depictions of the poetic images. The examples are numerous and, apart from the common titles and themes to be found throughout his paintings and poetry, it is interesting to compare chronologically the dates of the paintings with the period when the poems were written.

One can only conclude that there is more of a connection between his painting and poetry than Engonopoulos would have us believe. His often dismissive remarks concerning his poetry may owe something to his ever-present self-irony or, indeed, to a residue of bitterness left from its initial reception. Nevertheless, it would be impossible today to conceive of the artist Engonopoulos without the parallel dimension offered by his poetry.

All the constant themes in his poetry reappear in *In the Vale of Roseries*, though one theme stands out more than ever in this, the last collection published during his lifetime: the anthropocentric nature of his poetry. Man is at the center of both his poetry and painting, which reveals a deep respect for man, a deep sorrow at the often bitter consequences of his actions and yet the artist's need to communicate with him. As he put it himself in one of his interviews: "…man is the yardstick for every single thing: The measure of all things… Man is the subject of Hellenism. And it is for man that we create… In order to give him an outlet for his solitude; the strength, to abolish his solitude. Communication. This is what art offers…". What we have here is as clear a statement as any by Engonopoulos of the main aims of his artistic work, namely, his anthropocentric views, his concern with the essence of Hellenism and his concern with art as communication, above all, with art as a source of consolation. Throughout his long career, he made numerous statements to this effect in his essays on art and poetry: "If my life is devoted to painting and poetry, it's because painting and poetry both comfort and beguile me."; "If I devoted myself to art, I did it because life is so absurd that, if you don't have those means of escape to the selfless, it becomes unbearable."; and "The aim of the work of art is precisely to overcome this solitude."

Whether or not, through his painting and poetry, Engonopoulos succeeded in overcoming the solitude to which he refers and in finding the consolation he sought from art is not something open to scholarly investigation. What can be said, however, is that his poetry communicates today, in a way unimaginable fifty years ago, with younger readers in Greece as much if not more so than any other poet of his generation. It is full of Dionysian ecstasy, sensuality, profanity and outrage yet also of Apollonian nobleness, tenderness, humaneness and detachment. It has all the beauty, colour and light of Greece, yet remains enigmatic, iconoclastic and often disturbing. Perhaps the growing appeal of his work lies in the glimpses it offers of the absurdities and irony of human existence, of the mystery of life and death, of the marvel of love and beauty, and, perhaps above all, of the transformative magic of art.

David Connolly
Athens, 2019

Poems

ΠΟΛΥΞΕΝΗ

Βρυκόλακες ἀλαλάζοντες καί σιδηροπαγεῖς αὖραι μοῦ ἔφεραν χτές, περί τό μεσονύκτιον, μεσουρανοῦντος τοῦ ἡλίου τῆς δικαιοσύνης, τό μήνυμα τοῦ Ντάντε Γκαμπριέλ Ροσσέτη, τοῦ Isidore Ducasse* καί τοῦ Παναγῆ τοῦ Κουταλιανοῦ. Ἡ πίκρα μου στάθηκε μεγάλη! Μέχρι τῆς στιγμῆς ἐκείνης ἐπίστευα εἰς τά προφητικά ὁράματα τῶν τορναδόρων, πρόσμενα τούς χρησμούς τῶν ἀλλοφρόνων ἱππέων, προσδοκοῦσα τάς μεταφυσικάς ἐπεμβάσεις τῶν ἀγαλμάτων. Μέ γαλήνευε ἡ ἰδέα τοῦ πτώματός μου. Ἡ μόνη μου χαρά ἤτανε οἱ πλόκαμοι τῶν μαλλιῶν της. Ἔσκυβα εὐλαβικά καί φιλοῦσα τήν ἄκρια τῶν δακτύλων της. Παιδί ἀκόμα, στήν δύσιν τοῦ ἡλίου, ἔτρεχα ὡσάν τρελλός νά προφτάσω νά κλέψω, πρίν νυχτώσῃ, τά λησμονημένα σκιάχτρα μέσ' ἀπ' τά χωράφια. Καί ὅμως τήν ἔχασα, μπορῶ νά πῶ μέσ' ἀπό τά χέρια μου, ὡσάν νά μήν ἦταν ποτές παρά ἕνα ἀπατηλόν ὅραμα, παρά ἕνα κοινότατο σφυρί. Στή θέση της βρέθηκε μονάχα ἕνας καθρέπτης. Κι' ὅταν ἔσκυψα νά δῶ μέσα σ' αὐτόν τόν καθρέφτη, δέν εἶδ' ἄλλο τίποτες παρά μόνο δύο μικρά λιθάρια: τό ἕνα ἐλέγετο Πολυξένη, καί τό ἄλλο, Πολυξένη ἐπίσης.

* comte de Lautréamont

Παναγῆς Κουταλιανός. Ὁ περίφημος, ὑπερφυσικῶν δυνάμεων, Ἕλλην παλαιστής καί ἄλτης βαρῶν, ἀπό τήν Κούταλη τῆς Προποντίδος. Ἔχαιρε, παλαιά, παγκοσμίου φήμης καί μεγάλης δημοτικότητας ἀνάμεσα στόν ἑλληνικό λαό. Τό ὄνομά του ἦταν κοινό, στήν τρεχούμενη γλῶσσα, σάν ἤθελαν νά ποῦν γιά κανένα νέον Ἡρακλῆ. Κάτι τό παραπλήσιο μέ τόν κατοπινό Ἀργίτη Τζίμ Λόντο.

From: *Do Not Distract The Driver*

POLYXENI

Yesterday, around midnight, with the sun of justice at its zenith, shrieking ghouls and wrought-iron breezes brought me the message of Dante Gabriel Rossetti, Isidore Ducasse* and Panagis Koutalianos. My grief was immense! Till that moment I had believed in the lathe turners' prophetic visions, had awaited the frenzied knights' oracles, had expected the statues' metaphysical interventions. The idea of my corpse calmed me. My only joy was the plaits of her hair. I bowed devoutly and kissed her fingertips. When still a boy, at the setting of the sun, madly I would run to be in time, before night fell, to steal the forgotten scarecrows from out of the fields. And yet I lost her, from out of my very hands I might say, as though she were never more than a deceptive vision, never more than a common hammer. In her place there was only a mirror. And when I stooped to look in that mirror, I saw nothing but two small stones: the one was called Polyxeni, and the other, Polyxeni too.

* comte de Lautréamont

(Poet's note): Panagis Koutalianos. The renowned and superhumanly strong Greek wrestler and weightlifter from Koutali in the Propontis area. In the past, he enjoyed universal fame and was enormously popular among the Greek people. His name was used in common parlance to refer to someone with the attributes of a Hercules. Rather similar to the later Jim Londos from Argos.

ΑΜΑΖΟΝΕΣ

Ἡ «ὡραία Μαρίκα ἡ Πολίτισσα» ἦτο ἡ μόνη ἀναδεκτή τοῦ Πάπα Ἰννοκεντίου τοῦ VIII. Αὐτός ἦτο τότε μικρό παιδί, ἴσως μάλιστα καί νά μήν εἶχε γεννηθῆ ἀκόμη. Ἐκείνη ἦτο ἤδη πανδρεμένη, σύζυγος τοῦ ἐξ ἡγεμονικοῦ οἴκου Ἀρτάβαζου Σφυρικτρόπουλου, ἀνεψιοῦ — ἐπ' ἀδελφῇ — τοῦ Νῶε. Ὅμως, τό ἔγκλημα τοῦτο δέν ἠμποροῦσε νά μείνη χωρίς σκληράν τιμωρίαν, πρός παραδειγματισμόν. Πράγματι, ἀμέσως ἀπό τῆς ἑπομένης, ἐδόθη διαταγή εἰς ἱκανόν ἀριθμόν πλοίων νά πλεύσουν ἐσπευσμένως πρός τάς Καναρίους Νήσους καί τάς νήσους Φίτζιϊ, μέ τόν σκοπόν νά περισυλλέξουν ὅσον τό δυνατόν περισσοτέρας νεφέλας, χειμερινά ψεύδη, λησμονημένας ἀναμνήσεις, θανάσιμα ἁμαρτήματα καί βελόνας φωνογράφου, ἴσως ἀγγλικῆς κατασκευῆς. Τά περί οὗ ὁ λόγος πλοῖα ἦσαν ἐν ὅλῳ 7 τόν ἀριθμόν, δῆλα δή: 4 σακολέβες, 12 πρεγαντίνια, 2 βασιλικοί ντονανμάδες καί μία πεθαμένη ἀρρεβωνιαστικιά. Ὁ στόλος ἐπέρασε λίαν πρωΐ κάτω ἀπό τά παράθυρά μου. Ἔψαλλε ὕμνον ὡραιότατον, ἀλλά κάπως θλιμμένον καί μελαγχολικόν. Ἐνθυμοῦμαι ἀκόμη καί τώρα, ἀμυδρά βέβαια, τόν σκοπόν: ἦτο πολύ ἀνώτερος ἀπό χτύπημα κουδουνιοῦ, ἀλλά πάντως κατώτερος ἀπό σκούπα.

AMAZONS

"Fair Marika of Constantinople" was the only godchild of Pope Innocent VIII. He was at that time a small boy, in fact perhaps not even born yet. She was already espoused, wife to Artavazos Sphyriktropoulos, of noble lineage and nephew — on his sister's side — to Noah. However, this crime could not go without the severest of punishments, as an example to all. Indeed, the very next day, the order was given to a sizeable number of ships to sail in all haste to the Canary Isles and to the Isles of Fiji, with the aim of collecting as many clouds, winter falsehoods, forgotten memories, deadly sins and gramophone needles, perhaps made in England, as possible. The aforesaid ships totalled 7 in number, to wit: 4 spritsails, 12 brigantines, 2 royal dromonds, and a deceased fiancée. The fleet passed under my window early in the morning. It was singing a most beautiful hymn, though somewhat sad and melancholy. Even now I still remember, vaguely of course, the tune: it was superior to the ringing of a bell, but at any rate inferior to a broom.

ΙΣΩΣ

Βρέχει... Κι' ὅμως λυποῦμαι νά σᾶς τό πῶ: ἦταν, νά, ἕνα σπίτι, ἕνα μεγάλο θεώρατο σπίτι. Ἥτανε ἔρημο. Δέν εἶχε κανένα παράθυρο, κι' εἶχε ὅλο μπαλκόνια καί μιά μεγάλη καπνοδόχο. Ἐκεῖ καθόταν μιά κοπέλλα δίχως μάτια, πού ἀντίς γιά φωνή εἶχε ἕνα λουλούδι. Μέ ρώτησε:
— Μά τί εἴχατε καί καρφώνατε, ἔτσι, σήμερις ἀπό τό πρωΐ;
— Ἄ, τίποτες... τίποτες. Μιλοῦσα μέ τόν Ὅμηρο.
— Μέ τόν Ὅμηρο, τόν ποιητή;
— Ναί, μέ τόν Ὅμηρο τόν ποιητή, καί μ' ἕναν ἄλλο Ὅμηρο, ἀπ' τή Μοσχόπολη αὐτός, πού ἔζησε ὅλη του τή ζωή πάνου στά δέντρα, σάν πουλί, κι' ὅμως ἤτανε γνωστός σάν «ἄνθρωπος τοῦ γιοφυριοῦ» στίς γειτονιές κοντά στή λίμνη.

PERHAPS

It's raining... And yet I'm sorry to tell you: there was, over there see, a house; a large, a huge house. It was deserted. It had no window, had balconies all around and a large chimney. Sitting on it there was a girl without eyes, who instead of a voice had a flower. She asked me:

"Why were you hammering all morning like that, what was wrong with you?"

"Ah, nothing... nothing. I was talking to Homer."

"To Homer, the poet?"

'Yes, to Homer the poet, and also to another Homer, the one from Moschopolis, who lived all his life in the trees, like a bird, and yet was known as 'the bridge man' in the districts near the lake."

ΤΑ ΞΟΑΝΟΜΟΡΦΑ ΕΙΔΩΛΑ ΤΟΥ ΑΕΡΟΛΙΜΕΝΟΣ

ἔφυγαν γιά πάντα
μακριά μας
τά λιθάρια τῆς ἀνατολῆς
— ἐπιθαλάμιοι νεκροί κροκόδειλοι
μέσα στ' ἀνάκτορα
πού ἔβαψαν κίτρινα
οἱ ραπτομηχανές —
καί τώρα μένουν — καί θά μένουν αἰώνια — ἐδῶ
σάν ἀεροστεγῆ συμπεράσματα
τῆς πιό λεπτῆς Ἰθάκης
τ' ἀπόκρυφα ὀξύκεστρα τῶν πατροκτόνων
γιά νά ξυπνοῦνε μέσα μου
βαθιά — ὅταν γελῶ —
τά βρωμερά σεντόνια τῆς θυσίας

ὅπως τό δάσος πού θά βρῆ παρηγοριά στά σπέρματα
τῶν ψαριῶν τοῦ ὕπνου μέσ' στά χείλη
ζητεῖ τά συστηματικά πετρέλαια τῆς ζωῆς
καί λέει μονάχο τό τραγούδι
πού λέγαν τά μικρά παιδιά τά νυχτωμένα στό σοκάκι
γιά τά βελούδινα κοράλλια
τῶν ματιῶν

THE AIRPORT'S WOODEN IDOLS

gone for good
far from us
are the stones of the east
— dead epithalamic crocodiles
in palaces
dyed yellow
by sewing machines —
and remaining now — and remaining forever — here
like airtight conclusions
of the subtlest Ithaca
are the patricides' secret axes
to awaken within me
deep down — when I laugh —
the filthy sheets of sacrifice

just as the forest that will find solace in the sperm
of sleep's fish in the lips
seeks the systematic petroleum of life
and sings alone the song
sung in the lane by kiddies overtaken by night
about the velvet coral
of eyes

ΕΝΑΣ ΑΥΛΟΣ ΜΕΣ' ΣΤΗΝ ΑΥΛΗ ΤΗΣ ΕΚΑΤΟΜΒΗΣ

Ὁ νεκρός «γληγορεῖ» μέσα στή σκοτεινή τραπεζαρία. Γιά νά φτάση κανείς ὥς ἐκεῖ πρέπει νά περάση ἀπό μιάν ἀτέλειωτη σειρά σεντούκια γιομάτα βουλοκέρια. Ἐκεῖ γιομίζουν τά χέρια του ὅλο στεφάνια μέ πολύχρωμα λουλούδια, πού προορίζονται γιά τά κεφάλια τῶν ποιητῶν. Αὐτή εἶναι, ἄλλωστε, «ἡ ποίησις τοῦ δάσους», μέ κεχριμπάρια καί τυφλούς αὐλούς σά φεγγάρια. Ὁ νεκρός «γληγορεῖ» καί μετρᾶ συνεχῶς, ἀκούραστα: ἕνα, δύο, ἕνα, δύο. Ὅλη του ἡ προσπάθεια εἶναι ἕνας ψηλός τοῖχος, ὅλος κόκκινα τοῦβλα, μέ βουβή φωνή σάλπιγγος. Ποῦ καί ποῦ ν' ἀκουστῆ κι' ἕνα γέλιο, ἤ, ἀκόμη, κι' ἕνα τραγούδι, σά μαχαιριά, σάν τεφροδόχη. Ἄσκοπα, λέω τότες, ἄσκοπα περιπλανῶμαι στίς ἄδειες τρύπες τῶν ματιῶνε του. Τουλάχιστο, ἄν συνώδευε τίς ἀπεγνωσμένες μου κραυγές ἡ αἰολική ἅρπα τῆς χαρᾶς! Ἄν φύτρωνε στήν ἄκρη, στό κάθε δάχτυλο τῶν χεριῶν μου καί μιάν ὀρτανσία! Ἴσως τότες καί νά ἤτανε δυνατό νά μ' ἐξορίζανε βαθιά, μέσα στά πιό μουσικά λυχνάρια, μ' ἕνα βαρύ τόπι ὑφάσματος, σά γέλιο παιδιοῦ. Ὅμως, τίποτε... Τά πάντα εἰς μάτην. Ὁ νεκρός «γληγορεῖ» μ ό ν ο ς τ ο υ μέσα στή σκοτεινή τραπεζαρία.

From: *The Clavicembalos of silence*

A FLUTE IN THE HECATOMB YARD

The deceased remains "watchful" in the dim dining room. To get there one has to pass by an endless line of chests filled with sealing wax. There they fill his hands with wreaths of colourful flowers destined for the heads of poets. Besides, this is "the poetry of the forest", with amber and blind flutes like moons. The deceased remains "watchful" and constantly counts, tirelessly: one, two, one, two. His whole endeavour is a high wall, entirely of red bricks, with a bugle's mute voice. Every so often a peal of laughter may be heard, or, even, a song, like a knife stab, like an urn. Aimlessly, I reflect then, aimlessly I'm roaming in the empty sockets of his eyes. If only, at least, joy's aeolian harp were to accompany my desperate cries! If only a hydrangea were to sprout on the tip of my every finger! Perhaps then it would be possible for them to deeply exile me, in the most musical oil lamps, with a heavy bolt of cloth, like a child's laughter. Yet, nothing... All in vain. The deceased remains "watchful" a l l   a l o n e in the dim dining room.

ΑΛΕΞΙΒΡΟΧΙΑ

ἀπό καιρό τώρα
— κάθε νύχτα —
ἔρχεται ταχτικά
καί μέ βασανίζει
καί μέ σταυρώνει
καί μέ πληγώνει βαθιά
— θανάσιμα —
ἡ λέξις
«μπαϊράκι»
κι' ἀνησυχῶ
ἀγριεμένος
κι' ὅλο ρωτάω
μά τί νἆναι
τοῦτο πάλε
τί νά σημαίνη
ἄραγες
αὐτή
ἡ
καινούργια
ταραχή

μήπως εἶναι
τό μήνυμα
τοῦ θανάτου καί τῆς Χαρᾶς
τίποτες
κανένα δῶρο
τῆς θεᾶς

PARAPLUIES

for some time now
— every night —
coming regularly
to torment me
to crucify me
to wound me deeply
— mortally —
has been the word
"banner"
and I become anxious
roused
and constantly ask
but what's
all this again
what can be
the meaning
of
this
new
disturbance

is it perhaps
the message
of death and Joy
nothing
some gift
from the goddess

Δήμητρας
μήπως εἶναι
λέω πάλε
αὐτό πού λέν «λοστός (ἤ λωτός) — ζωστήρ»;

ἕνας κεραυνός πού ἔπεσε
μέσα
σ' ἕνα ποτήρι γάλα;

ἤ μήπως εἶναι
ἁπλούστερα
τά κλιμακωτά
πλοκάμια
μιᾶς ἱπποκάμπης
πού τραγουδᾶ
μέσα στά
πράσινα ἀνήλιαγα πάρκα
τοῦ βορρᾶ
μέ τίς λευκές
κολῶνες
τόν
κονιορτό
τῶν ἀγαλμάτων
καί τή νεκρή κοπέλλα
π' ἀγαπούσαμε ὅλοι
παράφορα
— σάν λουλούδι —
καί τήν ὠνομάζαμε
μέ τήν πονετική
λέξη

Demeter
is it perhaps
I again wonder
what they call a "jemmy (or gemmy) — girdle"?

a thunderbolt that fell
in
a glass of milk?

or is it perhaps
quite simply
the escalating
tentacles
of a hippocampus
singing
in
the green sunless parks
of the north
with the white
columns
the
dust cloud
of the statues
and the dead girl
whom we all loved
passionately
— like a flower —
whom we named
using the compassionate
word

«παράθυρο»
όταν ήμαστε μικρά
πολύ μικρά
παιδιά;

"window"
when we were small
very small
children?

ΣΤΑ ΟΡΗ ΤΗΣ ΜΥΟΥΠΟΛΕΩΣ

I

ὁ
δρόμος πρός τήν
ἀγάπη
εἶναι σπαρμένος
μάτια γατιῶν
μέσ' στό σκοτάδι
καί τή σιωπή
π' ἁπλώνεται γύρω
σά δίχτυ χαρᾶς
ὁ δρόμος πρός
τήν ἀγάπη
εἶναι νυχτερινός

πηγαίνει ψηλά
καί φτάνει
ἐκεῖ ὅπου
τό μπλέ
τοῦ κοβαλτίου
κι' ἀκόμη καί τό κίτρινο
— τοῦ καδμίου —
δέν εἶναι πιά τά χρώματα
μέ τά ὁποῖα
βάφω
τίς ζωγραφιές μου
ἀλλά λεπτές

ON THE MOUNTAINS OF MYOUPOLIS

I

the
path to
love
is strewn
with cats' eyes
in the darkness
and with the silence
that spreads all around
like a net of joy
the path to
love
is nocturnal

it rises high
and reaches
where
the blue
of cobalt
and even the yellow
— of cadmium —
are no longer the colours
with which
I paint
my pictures
but fine

μουσικές
άρπας
κινύρας
καί
σείστρων
φυγῆς

σείστρων
φυγῆς
σιγῆς
γῆς

II

οἱ τρελλές παρθένες
ἑνώθηκαν
μέσα στό δάσος
μέ τά δέντρα
— τόσες παρθένες
καί τόσα δέντρα —
ἥν ὥρα
τῆς μεγάλης
βροχῆς

οἱ μῆτρες τους ἤτανε
ἄσπιλες
— ἁγνές —
τόσο μετά
ὅσο καί πρίν

melodies
of harp
guitar
and
sistrums
gone

sistrums
gone
none
one

II

the mad maidens
merged
in the forest
with the trees
— so many maidens
and so many trees —
at the time
of the heavy
rain

their wombs were
immaculate
— chaste —
both after
and before

τήν καταιγίδα
τόσο μετά
ὅσο καί πρίν
τή συνουσία

κι' ὅμως
σάν ἔφυγαν τά σύννεφα
κι' ἔλαμψε
ὁ ἥλιος πάλι
ἔμενα πάντοτες
αἰχμάλωτος
μέσα στό σκοτεινό
σαλόνι
μέ τά κόκκινα βελοῦδα
καί τή βαρειά
κι' ἐπίμονη μυρωδιά
τῆς μούχλας
καί τῆς
ἡδονῆς

(ἀπ' τό παράθυρο
ἔβλεπα ἀτέλειωτες ταράτσες
— μέ μαρμάρινα κάγκελλα —
πού κατέβαιναν κάτω
ἴσαμε τή θάλασσα)

κι' ἤμουνα μ ό ν ο ς
μ' ἕναν μονάχα
— κι' αὐτόν μου ἄγνωστο —
ἄνθρωπο
σκυμμένο μέσ' στά σκοτάδια

the storm
both after
and before
the copulation

and yet
when the clouds went
and the sun
shone again
I was still
captive
in the dark
salon
with the red velvets
and the heavy
and persistent smell
of mildew
and
sensual pleasure

(from the window
I saw endless terraces
— with marble balustrades —
that reached down
as far as the sea)

and I was a l o n e
with just one
man
— he too unknown to me —
bent in the darkness

πάνου στά νεκρά πλῆκτρα
τοῦ κλειδοκύμβαλου
τῆς σιωπῆς

ἡ μούρη μου
ἤτανε φαγωμένη
σά λεπροῦ
— δέν φαινόνταν τίποτες πιά —
ἀπό τίς τύψεις
καί τήν πικρία
τῆς ἀγάπης

κι' ὅμως
ὁ ἄγνωστος
ἄνθρωπος
σηκώνονταν κάθε τόσο
ταχτικά
ἀπό τή σκοτεινή γωνιά του
καί μέ βασάνιζε ἀτάραχα
— ἀπ' τά χαράματα
ἴσαμε τό βράδυ —
καί πάνω στό μέτωπό μου
μέ πυραχτωμένα
μακριά σίδερα
μοῦγραφε συνεχῶς
αὐτές τίς λέξεις
— σά σύμβολο τρομερό —

«πατήρ — μήτηρ»
«ἀνήρ — γυνή»

over the dead keys
of the clavicembalo
of silence

my face
was eaten away
like a leper's
— nothing to see any more —
by the regrets
and the bitterness
of love

and yet
the unknown
man
got up every so often
at regular intervals
from his dark corner
and calmly tortured me
— from dawn
to dusk —
and on my brow
with long
glowing tongs
kept on writing
these words
— like some fearful symbol —

"father — mother"
"man — woman"

III

κοσμῶ τό μέτωπό
μου μέ
ψάρια κι' ὀμπρέλλες

βάζω μέσ' στά
μαλλιά μου
φωνές
φωτιᾶς

τά χέρια μου
γίνονται
οἱ σκουριασμένες
ἄγκυρες τῶν
ναυαγίων

κι' ἐνῶ ἁπλώνεται
— βαθμηδόν —
στ' ἀκρογιάλι
ἡ ἐρημιά
κι' ἡ νύχτα
βλέπω νά χάνωνται μακριά
— πάνω στή θάλασσα
στά βάθη τοῦ ὁρίζοντα —
τά τελευταῖα φῶτα
τ ο ῦ
χ α μ ο ῦ

III

I adorn
my brow with
fish and umbrellas

in my hair
I put
cries
of fire

my arms
become
the rusted
anchors of
shipwrecks

and while over the shore
— gradually —
descends
desolation
and the night
I see disappearing far off
— on the sea
in the depths of the horizon —
the last lights
o f
l o s s

ΣΥΝΕΠΕΙΑ

ἡ βυθοκόρος
τῶν ὀνείρων
λειτουργεῖ
μόνον
μέ τήν προσθήκη
τῶν λέξεων
«τρυγόνα μου περήφανη»
κατόπιν
— βέβαια —
τῆς εἰδικῆς ἀδείας
τοῦ τελευταίου
ἀλεξανδρινοῦ γλύπτου
— καί φιλοσόφου —
τῶν πρώτων μεταχριστιανικῶν
χρόνων

ὅμως
τ' ἀποτελέσματα
εἶναι μᾶλλον
ἀξιοδάκρυτα
— καί ἀπολύτως κατακριτέα —
ὅταν λάβουμε
μάλιστα ὑπ' ὄψει
ὅτι τό ὅλον ἔργο τοῦ
φημισμένου αὐτοῦ γλύπτου
εἶναι δέν εἶναι

CONSEQUENCE

the dredger
of dreams
operates
only
with the addition
of the words
"my proud turtle dove"
following
— naturally —
special permission
from the last
Alexandrian sculptor
— and philosopher —
of early post-Christian
times

yet
the results
are rather
pitiable
— and completely reprehensible —
when moreover
we consider
that the entire work
of this renowned sculptor
is at most

μισή δωδεκάδα
βοῦρτσες τῶν δοντιῶν

ὅταν σκεφτοῦμε πώς
ὅλη του ἡ φιλοσοφία
συνοψίζεται
σέ τρεῖς ἀρμαθιές
κλειδιά
κρεμασμένες
σέ τρία διαφορετικά
δέντρα
ἀνάμεσα στά
χείλη
τά δόντια
καί τά στήθη
τῆς Ὑπατίας

κι' ὅταν
τέλος
ὁμολογήσουμε
ὅτι βυθοκόρος
πραγματικά
δέν ὑπάρχει
καί πώς
μ' αὐτή τή λέξη
ἐννοούσαμε
— ἐνίοτε —
τίς καπνοδόχες
πού ξεμαλλιάζει

half a dozen
toothbrushes

when we reflect that
his whole philosophy
is summed up
in three bunches
of keys
hanging
from three different
trees
between the
lips
the teeth
and the breasts
of Hypatia

and when
finally
we admit
that the dredger
in reality
doesn't exist
and that
by this word
we meant
— sometimes —
the chimney stacks
dishevelled

ὁ ἄνεμος
τοῦ φθινοπώρου
πάνω
στίς
στέγες
τῶν σπιτιῶν

by the wind
of autumn
up
on
the roofs
of the houses

ΠΡΩΪΝΟ ΤΡΑΓΟΥΔΙ*

ἐρώτησα
κάποτες γιατί
τάχατες
ἡ τραγική
καί σεμνή παρθένα
πού λέγονταν Πουλχερία
τήν παραμονή τοῦ
γάμου της
σφουγγάρισε προσεχτικά ὅλο
τό σπίτι
καί τήν ἑπομένη
ἀπέθανε;

μιά
πού καθάρισε καί νοικοκέρεψε
τά πάντα
γιατί δέ χάρηκε
κι' αὐτή
τίς μακρυές λευκές νταντέλλες,
τούς λευκούς πολύπλοκους φαρμπαλάδες
καί τά πολύχρωμα
μεγάλα
φτερά
τοῦ γάμου;
γιατί

* aubade, σαμπαῖ, εωθινόν

MORNING SONG*

I asked
once why
apparently
the tragic
and demure maiden
by the name of Pulcheria
on the eve of
her wedding
diligently mopped all
the house
and the next day
died?

Since
she had cleaned and tidied
everything
why didn't she too
delight in
the long white laces
the intricate white frills
and the large
colourful
feathers
of the wedding?
why

* aubade, sabahı, reveille

ἐναπόθεσε ἔτσι σιωπηλά
χάμω στά
σανίδια
τή μεγάλη κίτρινη πεταλούδα
καί τά χάρτινα λουλούδια
πού ἤτανε μέσα
στό κεφάλι της;
τό μπαλσαμωμένο
πουλί
πού ἤτανε μέσα στό κλουβί
τοῦ θώρακά
της;

γιατί;

διότι
— εἶπε ἴσως ὁ πατέρας μου —

διότι
πρέπει νά ἔχη
ὁ στρατιώτης τό τσιγάρο του
τό μικρό παιδί
τήν κούνια του
κι' ὁ ποιητής
τά
μανιτάρια
του

διότι πρέπει
νά ἔχη

did she silently place
down on the
floorboards
the large yellow butterfly
and the paper flowers
that were inside
her head?
the stuffed
bird
that was inside the cage
of
her chest?

why?

because
— so my father said perhaps —

because
the soldier has to have
his cigarette
the little child
his cradle
and
the poet
his
mushrooms

because the condottiere
has to have

ὁ στραδιώτης τήν
πλεκτάνη του
τό μικρό παιδί
τόν τάφο του
ὁ ποιητής τή
ροκάνα
του

διότι πρέπει
νά ἔχῃ
ὁ στραθιώτης
τό σκεπάρνι του
τό μικρό παιδί τό
βλέμμα του
ὁ ποιητής
τό
ροκάνι του

Τό «Πρωϊνό Τραγούδι» εἶναι ἡ ἀληθινή, καί θλιβερή, ἱστορία μιᾶς σεμνῆς Ραιδεστινῆς κόρης, πού γνώρισα στά πολύ παιδικά μου χρόνια. *Στρατιώτης.* Ὁ πατέρας μου ἔστεκε ἀνένδοτος νά μοῦ στέλνῃ ἕνα μικρό χαρτζιλίκι σάν ἤμουνα κληρωτός. «Πρέπει νά ἔχῃ ὁ σ τ ρ α τ ι ώ τ η ς τό τσιγάρο του!» ἔλεγε. *Στραδιώτης.* Μισθοφόρος τῶν «ἑλληνικῶν ταγμάτων» στήν ὑπηρεσία τῶν μεγάλων Condottieri τῆς Ἀναγεννήσεως. Σήμερα ἀκούγεται, στήν Ἰταλία, σάν ὄνομα οἰκογενειακό. *Στραθιώτης.* Λέξις τῆς κρητικιᾶς διαλέκτου, μέ τή σημασία τοῦ ὁδοιπόρος.

his
ploy
the little child
his tomb
the poet
his
rattle

because the wayfarer
has to have
his
adze
the little child
his gaze
the poet
his
rasp

(Poet's note): "Morning Song" is the true and sad story of a demure Raidestini girl, whom I knew in my early childhood.

(Poet's note): Soldier (Greek: *stratiotis*). My father was always adamant about sending me a small amount of pocket money when I was doing my national service. "The s o l d i e r has to have his cigarette" he would say. Condottiere (Greek: *stradiotis*). A mercenary in the Greek regiments in the service of the great Condottieri in the Renaissance. Today, it can be found in Italy as a family name. Wayfarer (Greek: *strathiotis*). A word in Cretan dialect meaning wayfarer.

ΤΟ ΤΡΑΓΟΥΔΙ ΕΝΟΥ ΣΤΡΑΤΙΩΤΗ

ὁ μαῦρος ἀγέρας
ξεκινάει τρελλός
ἀπό τά σκοτεινά
λημέρια
του
μουγκρίζει
σά θεριό
περνώντας
ἀπ' τά ἔρημα
στενά σοκάκια
κι' ὁρμᾶ μέσ' ἀπ' τίς
ξεχαρβαλωμένες
πόρτες
— πού δέν
τίς μανταλώνουν πιά
τά σουγλερά
καρφιά
τῶν πόθων μου —
χυμάει ἀβάσταχτος
ἀπό τίς
ξύλινες
ἐρειπωμένες
σκάλες
πού κλαῖνε
γοερά
— μ' ἀνθρώπινες φωνές
σάν ἄρπα αἰολικιά —

From: *The return of the birds*

A SOLDIER'S SONG

    the black wind
    sets out wildly
    from its
    dark
    lairs
    bellows
    like a beast
    passing
    through the empty
    narrow lanes
    and surges through the
    unhinged
    doors
    — that are
    no longer fastened
    by the sharp
    bolts
    of my desires —
    rushes unrestrainable
    up the
    rickety
    wooden
    staircases
    that cry
    plaintively
    — with human voices
    like an aeolian harp —

ξεσπάει μέσ' στά
πελώρια
νεκρά δωμάτια
σφυράει
ξεφεύγοντας
μέσ' ἀπό τίς
καπνοδόχες
καί
τίς
ρωγμές τοῦ ταβανιοῦ

— ἀφοῦ παρέσυρε μαζύ του
τόν καπνό τῶν ξύλων
πού καῖνε
κάπου
κρυφά
μέσ' στίς χορταριασμένες
ἄδειες
αὐλές —

καί ξεπετιέται
ψηλά στά οὐράνια
κι' ἀναμαλλιάζει
τά μαῦρα σύγνεφα

ταράζει
ἀλλάζει
στό ἄπειρο
τίς
βουβές

bursts through the
enormous
dead rooms
whistles
escaping
through the
chimneys
and
the
cracks in the ceiling

— after sweeping away with it
the smoke of the wood
being burnt
somewhere
secretly
in the overgrown
deserted
yards —

and leaps
high into the heavens
and ruffles
the black clouds

upsets
offsets
in the infinite
those
silent

ἀπειλές
τους
καί
ξανακατεβαίνει
μ' ἑλιγμούς
φιδίσιους
πρός
τήν
ἀκρολιμνιά

κι' ἔρχεται
ἡ φριχτή ὁρμή
του
καί σπᾶ
καί τσακίζεται
στή νικηφόρα
 ἀντίσταση
στίς
λεῦκες
τίς λευκές
τίς ψιλόλιγνες
μέ τίς
μυριάδες τίς
φωνές
στά μαῦρα
τά θλιμμένα
τά
καβάκια
τά
σιωπηλά

threats
of theirs
and
descends again
with twists
and twirls
towards
the
lakeside

and its
terrible force
comes
and beats
and breaks
against the victorious
resistance
of the
poplars
white ones
and slender
with the
myriads
of voices
on the black
the
sorrowful
the
silent
coves

κι' ἡ μαύρη λίμνη
μνήσκει
ἀτάραχη
μέ τά μαῦρα
τά κρεμάμενα
νερά της
τούς μαύρους
θρύλλους της
τίς ὄχθες της
τίς μαῦρες
τίς ἀπόγκρεμνες
τά ἔρμα
της τζαμιά
τό γκρέμνιο
τό στρατῶνα
τ' ἄροτρα
τούς βράχους
τίς λευκές
ἁρμονικές
γυναῖκες
μέ τό βλέμμα
τό πικρό
τῆς
ἱκεσίας

πού γώ
ξερρίζωσα
βαθειά
τά μάτια τους
σάν μ' ἕνα

and the black lake
threatens
unperturbed
with its black
its hanging
waters
its black
legends
its black
steep
shores
its deserted
mosques
the ruined
barracks
the ploughs
the rocks
the white
harmonious
women
with the bitter
look
of
supplication

for I
rooted
out
their eyes
when with

τέτοιον
ὅμοιο καιρό
ἐθαλασσόδερνα κάποτε
— μ' ἐνάντιον ἄνεμο —
κάτω
κατά
τά
μέρη
τῆς
Μονεβασιᾶς

just
such weather
I was once buffetted
— by a contrary wind —
down
in
those
parts
around
Monemvasia

Η ΕΡΩΤΙΚΗ ΠΛΕΚΤΑΝΗ

ἡ βροχή πάει νά κοπάση
— νἄρθη ὁ σεισμός; —
οἱ βρυκολάκοι ἐβαλθῆκαν νά χτυποῦνε τά κουδούνια
 ἐνῶ οἱ καρδιές στάζουνε αἷμα
μέσα στά σκοτεινά φαράγγια
σ' ἄξενες κοιλάδες
τῆς ἄρνησης μιά ὅπου χάθηκε τό ἄστρο
ὁ συνοδίτης
στῶν Νοτιάδων τά λημέρια
τό Ἄργος

πόσο θά ἤθελα νά τήν ξανάβλεπα
— «ὡς ἦτο» —
πρίν ἔρθ' ἡ νύχτα
καί μᾶς πάρη στό βυθό της
πρίν τά σαλπίσματα τῆς τρικυμίας
ἀναγγείλουν
πώς ἐραστής παρθένων
εἴταν ὁ δύτης

στῶν τράγων τῶν ἱερῶν τό βαρύ βλέμμα μαζεύτηκαν
ξανά τά μαῦρα σύννεφα τῆς μπόρας:
οἱ πράσινες οἱ φυλλωσιές ὅπου γυαλίζουν στά σκοτάδια
ὅλη τή νύχτα ἔχουνε πάλι νά παλέψουν
μέ τά ραπίσματα
τό μῖσος
τῆς βροχῆς τό πεῖσμα

LOVE'S SNARE

the rain has almost ceased
— is the earthquake coming? —
the ghouls have taken to ringing bells
while the hearts drip blood
in the dark ravines
in inhospitable valleys
of negation since the star vanished
the escort
in the Southerlies' lairs
Argos

how I would like to see her again
— "as she was" —
before night comes
and takes us to its depths
before the tempest's trumpeting
announces
that the maidens' lover
was the diver

the storm's black clouds again gathered
in the sacred goats' grave gaze:
the green foliage that shines in the darkness
all night long again has to wrestle
with the blows
the hate
the rain's persistence

(πλάγι στή λάμπα ὅπ' ἀνάψαμε
νά μή χαθοῦμε
τό μυστικό τριαντάφυλλο ἀνθίζει)

σίμωσ' ἐδῶ κοντά στό παραθύρι
καί παραμέρισε τούς σκοτεινούς βαρεῖς μπερντέδες
κύττα
οἱ βρυκόλακες ἐφτάξαν
στό ἀκρογιάλι
ἐκεῖ στό ξύλινο σπιτάκι ὅπου κατώκει
ἕνας ἀρχαῖος θεός
ἰχθυοτρόφος
κι' ἀφοῦ χυθήκανε μέσα στούς κρύφιους ἀρσανάδες
σκαριά καινούργια ἐσκαρφιστήκανε νά στήσουν
γιά νάν τά ρίξουνε στή θάλασσα
ν ά   φ ύ γ ο υ ν

«Σεισμό» ὠνόμασαν τό πρῶτο τους τρικάταρτο καράβι

(beside the lantern that we lit
not to get lost
blooms the secret rose)

come here next to the window
and draw aside the dark heavy curtains
look
the ghouls have reached
the shore
that small wooden hut where dwells
an ancient god
a fish farmer
and after rushing into the hidden boatyards
they contrived to build new craft
to cast into the sea
a n d   f l e e

"Earthquake" was what they named their first
　threemaster

ΤΟ ΕΒΔΟΜΟ ΤΡΑΓΟΥΔΙ ΤΗΣ ΑΓΑΠΗΣ

οἱ φωταψίες τοῦ ἔρωτα
σάν ἄνεμος ὠτακουστής σέ σύννεφο διαβατικό
λές καί τό κρύσταλλο τῶν τραγικῶν ματιῶν σου
τά μακρυά μαλλιά σου μέχρι τά κύματα τῆς ἀκρογιαλιᾶς
τά δέσαν ἄστρα σέ βράχια ἁρμονικά
ὀπτασίες στήν προσευχή πού δέονται τά φύκια
στό γαλάζιο κοντύλι τ' οὐρανοῦ
μέχρι κεῖ κάτω στῶν ζωντανῶν χειλιῶν σου τό χάδι
πετοῦν τά πουλιά σέ τραγούδια ὑακίνθων
τά ἄμφια τῆς ὀροσειρᾶς νυχτώνουν ὑποσχέσεις
ὑποσχέσεις ζωῆς καί χαρᾶς καί ζωῆς καί χαρᾶς
ὄργανο τῆς μουσικῆς λαχτάρας στά δάχτυλά σου
μέ τοῦ ὕπνου τή φοβέρα καί τήν ἰαχή
σύθαμπο ὀνείρου πέρ' ἀπ' τά σκέλη τά λεπτά μέ ἀνταύ-
    γειες ρόδων
στή σκάλα τῆς ἡδονῆς ὅλο καί πιό τρελλά
ὀρθώσου τριφύλλι γιοφύρι παλμῶν ψαλμῶν σπασμῶν
σέ σώματα διάφανα — μέ λαμπρότητα κρίνων — πού
    τόσο ἐβασάνισ' ἡ δίψα
σέ σύμβολα ὅρμων θά σημάνη ὁ ἥλιος ὡς θά 'ρθῆ νά κο-
    πάση ὁ πόθος
μακρυά ταξιδεύουν τοῦ βραδιοῦ οἱ στερνές ἀναμνήσεις
— πῶς ἀλλιῶς νά ἱστορηθοῦν τά κρυφά τοῦ ἀγέρα τρα-
    γούδια
τά τραγούδια πού εἶχες πεῖ καί θά πῆς καί θά ζήσης
σ' ἀδεή προσμονή στῆς λατρείας τή φλόγα

LOVE'S SEVENTH SONG

love's luminescense
like an eavesdropping wind on a passing cloud
as though the crystal of your tragic eyes
your long hair as far as the waves on the shore
were bound by the stars to harmonious rocks
visions in the prayer the seaweed offers
on the sky's azure slate
as far as down on your vibrant lips' caresses
the birds soar in songs of hyacinths
night falls on the mountain's vestments promises
promises of life and joy and life and joy
instrument of musical longing on your fingers
with sleep's dread and cry
dream's dusk beyond the delicate legs with hues of
    roses
ever more crazy on pleasure's scale
rise clover over balms psalms qualms
on transparent bodies — with the brightness of lilies
    — so tormented by thirst
on symbols of bays the sun will sound till longing
    abates
the last recollections of evening travel afar
— how else might the wind's secret songs be re-
counted
the songs you had sung and will sing and will live
in unawed expectation in worship's flame

οἱ φωτεινές σου παλάμες τούς ὁρίζοντες σμίγουν
ἡ φωνή σου θωπεύει τή δροσιά πού ἁπλώνει ἡ δύσις
τό κορμί σου δονεῖ στά θερμά παρακάλια τῆς νύχτας

καί στό βλέμμα σου ἠχεῖ ἡ χαρά;

your radiant palms unite the horizons
your voice caresses the chill spread by the sunset
your body pulsates to night's warm entreaties

and does joy resound in your gaze?

Η ΤΕΛΕΥΤΑΙΑ ΕΜΦΑΝΙΣΙΣ ΙΟΥΔΑ ΤΟΥ ΙΣΚΑΡΙΩΤΗ

Ἡ μικρή ἀμερικανική πόλις, ἡ χαμένη μέσα στίς ἀπέραντες ἐκτάσεις τῶν πεδιάδων τοῦ Ἄϋρτον, ἔχασε αὐτή τή βαθειά γαλήνη στήν ὁποία εἴτανε συνηθισμένη ἀπό τίς μέρες, τίς πρόσφατες ἄλλωστε — γύρω στά 1867 —, τῆς ἱδρύσεώς της. Ταχτικά περί τά μεσάνυχτα, ἄνθρωπος, παράξενος καί σκοτεινός, εἰσέδυε καί στά πιό καλοαμπαρωμένα σπίτια ἀκόμα, ἐτάραζε τόν ὕπνο τῶν κοιμωμένων, ἀναστάτωνε τίς ἤσυχες συνειδήσεις, πίκραινε θανάσιμα τίς καρδιές, καί μέ μιάνα μεταλλική φλογέρα, πού ἔπαιζε στήν ἐντέλεια, ξύπναγε σ' ὅλους μιάν ἔντονη, τυραννική ὅσο κι' ἀκαθόριστη, νοσταλγική διάθεση. Περιττό νά προστεθῇ πώς κανείς δέν ἐθυμότανε τίποτε, μόλις ξημέρωνε, ἀπό τό φοβερό βραχνά. Ὅμως, ὅλη τή μέρα, λές κι' ἕνα μεγάλο βάρος ἐπλάκωνε τίς ψυχές. Κάποιος νυχτοπερπατητής ἔλυσε τό βασανιστικό τοῦτο μυστήριο. Μιά νύχτα ὅπου, ὅλως κατά τύχη, τόν ἔφεραν τ' ἀβέβαια βήματά του ἐπί λόφου ἐξοχικοῦ, δεσπόζοντος τῆς πόλεως, ἀντελήφθη ὅτι τό μπρούντζινο ἄγαλμα τοῦ Ἀβραάμ Λίνκολν πού εἴταν στημένο ἐκεῖ πάνω ἔλειπε, καί τό μαρμάρινο βάθρο φάνταζε ἔρημο κι' ἐγκαταλελειμμένο κάτω ἀπό τό φῶς τῶν προβολέων. Ὁ «Πρόεδρος», ὁ χάλκινος αὐτός Ἀβραάμ Λίνκολν, ἦτο λοιπόν ὁ νυχτερινός παράξενος καί σκοτεινός ἐπισκέπτης! Ὁ καταδότης ἠμείφθη μέ ποσόν τι δολλαρίων. Ἐρωτηθείς, ὠνομάζετο Ἰούδας. Τό ἐπώνυμον δέ, Ἰσκαριώτης.

THE LAST APPEARANCE OF JUDAS ISCARIOT

The small American town, buried in the vast expanses of the Ayrton plains, lost that deep peace to which it had been accustomed since the days, not too long before — around 1867 — of its founding. Regularly at around midnight, a man, both strange and sombre, entered into even the most well-bolted homes, disturbing the sleep of the inhabitants, stirring their untroubled consciences, mortally embittering their hearts, and with a tin flute that he played to perfection, he awoke in them all a deep sense of nostalgia, at once vague and oppressive. Needless to say that with the break of day no one remembered anything of the horrible nightmare. Yet throughout the day it was as though a great weight lay upon their hearts. A certain nighttime stroller solved this baffling mystery. One night when, quite fortuitously, his uncertain steps led him to a hill overlooking the town, he noticed that the bronze statue of Abraham Lincoln that had been erected there was missing, and the marble pedestal appeared desolate and abandoned in the glare of the floodlights. So the "President", that bronze Abraham Lincoln, was then the strange and sombre nocturnal visitor! The informer was rewarded with a sum of dollars. He answered to the name of Judas. His surname, Iscariot.

«ΕΝΘΥΜΙΟΝ ΤΗΣ ΚΩΝΣΤΑΝΤΙΝΟΥΠΟΛΕΩΣ»

L.N.

πάνω εἰς τή μαρμάρινη τήν προκυμαία τοῦ ἀνακτόρου
ἐναποθέσανε σέ διαστήματα ὡς ἔγγιστα κανονικά
ψηλούς σωρούς τά ξύλα
πού ἐφέραν τά καΐκια ἀπό τά μακρυνά
παράλια δάση

κι' ἄλλοι σωροί εἶναι ἀπό ψιλούς
λεπτούς κορμούς σάν κορμί κόρης
κι' ἄλλοι σωροί ἀπό
θεώρατα μεγάλα
δέντρα

καί βρέχει συνεχῶς καί ἡ ἐπίμονη βροχή μουσκεύει
τ' ἄχαρα τά ξύλα
καί γυαλίζουνε τά μάρμαρα τοῦ πλακοστρώτου
καθώς τό νερό ἀτέλειωτα τά πλένει καί τά ξαναπλένει

κι' ὁ οὐρανός βαρύς μαζύ καί μαῦρος
— ἄραγες ποιός ξέρει τί ὥρα τῆς ἡμέρας νἄναι; —
καμμιάν ἐλπίδα δέ στέργει γιά νά δώση

(ἡ ἀπέναντι ὄχθη ἔχει χαθῆ
λές δέν ὑπῆρξε)

κι' ἡ θάλασσα εἶναι μουντή κι' ἀγριεμένη

"SOUVENIR OF CONSTANTINOPLE"

L.N.

on the palace's marble wharf
at nearly regular intervals they placed
in tall stacks the timber
brought by the caïques from faraway
coastal forests

and some stacks are of thin
slender trunks like a young girl's body
and other stacks are of
huge great
trees

and it's ever raining and the persistent rain soaks
the drab timber
and the marble flagstones glisten
as the water endlessly washes and washes them again

and the sky at once heavy and dark
— who knows what time of day it is? —
deigns not to offer any hope

(the opposite shore has vanished
as though it didn't exist)

and the sea is turbid and rough

σάν οἱ πυκνές οἱ στάλες τῆς βροχῆς πού τή βαρᾶνε
νἄχουν ξυπνήσει μέσα της μιά μάνητα τεράστια
πού μέ τί κόπο τηνέ
συγκρατάει

ἄλλος κανείς σέ τοῦτο τό ἐρημικό τοπίο δέ μοιάζει νἆναι
πάρεξ μονάχα ἐγώ — ὁ ἴδιος —
ὀρθός ὡς στέκω μέ τά κόκκινα μαλλιά μου μουσκεμένα
νά κολλοῦνε ἀπάνω εἰς τό μέτωπό μου

τῆς ἀγάπης τά βάσανα μ' ἔχουνε φέρει στό εὐγενικό τό
    περιγιάλι
κι' ὅλο ὁ νοῦς μου εἶναι σέ μιάν ὑπέροχη
ὑπερήφανη μαγνόλια
ὅπου σ' αυτά τά μέρη ἐδῶ
θάλλει κι' ἀνθίζει

as if the dense raindrops assailing it
have awakened in it great wrath
that with what toil
it holds in check

there seems to be no one in this desolate place
save me alone — myself —
standing erect with my red hair soaked
and sticking to my brow

love's torments have brought me to this noble
    shore
and my mind is ever on an exquisite
haughty magnolia
that here in these parts
flourishes and blooms

ΑΠΑΤΡΙΣ ΑΠΕΛΑΥΝΟΜΕΝΟΣ ΒΙΑΙΑ

Ἔτσι ὀρθός καθώς ἐστέκετο, μέ τά ὡραῖα μακρυά ξανθά μαλλιά του ν' ἁπλώνωνται κυματιστά πάνω εἰς τούς ὤμους του, ἔμορφος, ὑψηλός, μέ περικεφαλαίαν, νεκρόφιλος κι' ἀριστοτελικός, μέ κηρύκειον Ἑρμοῦ νέου στό δεξί χέρι, ἔμοιαζε ἴδιος ἄγαλμα ἀρχαίου θεοῦ. Ὁσάκις ἐπρόκειτο περί πλατείας, πάντα εἴτανε πλάγι του μία ὁλόγυμνη ὡραία κόρη, μέ κορμί χρυσό κι' ἁπαλό σά κεχριμπάρι, τά μαλλιά της μακρυά, μαῦρα, ν' ἀγγίζουνε καταγῆς, μέ ἥλιο καί φεγγάρι ζωγραφισμένα ἐπί τῶν μαστῶν της, μέ μικρόν ὁμοίωμα ἀηδόνος ἐπί τοῦ φύλου, καί δύο, τρία τριαντάφυλλα κόκκινα ραμμένα ἐντέχνως ἕνα στό κάθε γόνατο. Ὁσάκις ἐπρόκειτο περί μικρᾶς στενωποῦ, πλάγι του, καθημένη κόρη, κι' αὐτή ὁλόγυμνη, ξανθιά ὅμως, μέ φυσαρμόνικα καί βοϊδοκεφαλή. Σέ προβλήτα λιμανιοῦ, ἡ κόρη: κοκκινομαλλοῦσα, ὑπερήφανη, μέ δέρμα λεπτό κι' ἄσπρο σάν τό χιόνι, μέ τό ὄνομά της Α ὐ λ η τ ρ ί ς γραμμένο σέ διάφορα μέρη τοῦ σώματος μέ ποικιλόχρωμες λαδομπογιές. Πλησίον λίμνης: ἡ κόρη μέ ἄρπα. Πλησίον δάσους: ἡ κόρη μέ σάρπα. Νύχτα ἐντός καπηλείου: ἡ κόρη ὡραία, ἀγέρωχη καί σχεδόν ἡμιθανής, μέ πολυτελεστάτην ἀμφίεση πράσινου μεταξωτοῦ, μέ βεντάλια σέ σχῆμα ρεματιᾶς ἤ 7, νά χορεύη χορούς ἔξαλλους καί συμβολικούς. Τήν ἡμέρα, αὐτός καί ἡ κόρη ἀσχολοῦντο μέ τήν πάλη τῆς ζωῆς. Τή νύχτα, ἀσχολοῦντο μέ τήν πάλη τοῦ ἔρωτα. Αὐτός ἔβγανε μιά πελώρια μαχαίρα, τῆς τήν ἔμπηγε βαθειά στό στῆθος, καί τήν τραβοῦσε ἴσια κάτω. Βύθιζε ἀργά τά χέρια — ἡ κόρη πάντα ξαπλωμένη στό

STATELESS FORCIBLY DEPORTED

Standing erect as he was, with his lovely long fair hair flowing in waves over his shoulders, comely, tall, with helmet, a necrophile and Aristotelian, with the caduceus of a young Hermes in his right hand, he looked like a statue of an ancient god. Whenever it concerned a square, beside him he always had a beautiful stark naked girl with a body of gold and soft like amber, her hair long and black, down to the ground, with a sun and moon painted on her breasts, with the tiny image of a nightingale on her pubes and two or three red roses adroitly stitched one on each knee. Whenever it concerned a narrow lane, beside him was a girl sitting down, stark naked too, but blonde, with a mouthorgan and bovine head. On the harbour's quay, the girl: red-haired, proud, with skin delicate and white like snow, with the name F l u t e - g i r l inscribed on various parts of her body in a variety of coloured oil paints. Beside a lake: a girl with a harp. Beside a wood: a girl with a wrap. Nighttime in the inn: a beautiful girl, haughty and virtually half-dead, in luxurious attire of green silk, with a fan in the shape of a ravine or a 7, dancing delirious and symbolic dances. During the daytime, he and the girl engaged in life's struggle. During the nighttime, in love's struggle. He would take out a huge knife, plunge it deep into her breast, and drag it straight downwards. He slowly immersed his hands — with the girl ever reclining on the bed — and pulled out ribbons, green ones,

κρεββάτι — καί τραβοῦσε ὄξω κορδέλλες πράσινες, κόκκινες, κίτρινες, γαλάζιες, παρδαλές, ἀνάκατα, καί τίς σήκωνε ψηλά, σέ ὡραῖο σχῆμα προσφορᾶς. Μέσ' ἀπ' τά κουβάρια βγαῖναν περιστέρια, πού πετοῦσαν πρῶτα ἀβέβαια, φοβισμένα, κι' ὕστερα δίναν μιά, ἴσια κατά τόν οὐρανό. Τώρα ἡ βάρκα. Νά κατεβῆ στή βάρκα. Κατέβαινε στή βάρκα, ἔμπαινε, ἔπιανε τά κουπιά, ὀρθός, κι' ἔλαμνε βιαστικά. Ἡ κόρη, γυμνή, μά ναί: πάντα γυμνή, στέκονταν πίσω του, καί περνοῦσε θωπευτικά τούς ὡραίους βραχίονες γύρω στό λαιμό του.

red ones, yellow ones, blue ones, mottled ones, pell-mell, and lifted them high, in a wonderful show of offering. From out of the tangle came doves, which at first flew uncertainly, frightened, and then took off, straight into the sky. Now the boat. To go down to the boat. He went down to the boat, got in, took up the oars, standing erect, and rowed hurriedly. The girl, naked, ah yes: ever naked, stood behind him, and caressingly wrapped her lovely arms around his neck.

ΚΑΦΦΕΝΕΙΑ ΚΑΙ ΚΟΜΗΤΕΣ ΥΣΤΕΡΑ ΑΠΟ ΤΑ ΜΕΣΑΝΥΧΤΑ

οἱ ταξιδιῶτες ἦρθαν κι' ἔφυγαν
κεκηρυγμένοι ἐχθροί τῆς ἴδιας λησμονιᾶς καί τοῦ ἴδιου
    πάθους
ὑλοτόμοι πάντα τοῦ ἴδιου πόθου
καί μπροστά τους ν' ἁπλώνωνται ὅσο παίρνει τό μάτι κι'
    ἡ καρδιά
τά ἴδια μαῦρα κουρελιασμένα σύννεφα
νά μπλέχουν τά κατάρτια τους
νά σκουριάζουνε τίς ἄγκυρές τους
νάν τούς σφυρᾶν κρυφά μέσα στ' αὐτί μέ τή μπουρού
τήν ἴδια ὀδύνη

λές ἕνα κίτρινο χρυσό
λαμπερό
νά βάψη αὐτό τό μαῦρο αἰσχρό καί θλιβερό τοπίο
πού τό τρυποῦν σκληρά
τά νυσταγμένα φῶτα τῶν ἠλεκτρικῶν λαμπτήρων
τά νυσταγμένα φῶτα μιᾶς ἀξιοδάκρυτης — ἰδανικῆς —
    πορνείας
καί τῆς ψωριάρικιας γκαμήλας τό νυσταλέο τό «che vuoi?»

λές;

σκέψου πώς εἶν' ἀδύνατο
πώς εἶναι κι' ἀπολύτως περιττό νά ξεφωνίσης καί νά πῆς
    ὅλη τούτη τή φλόγα

From: *Eleusis*

CAFÉS AND COMETS
AFTER MIDNIGHT

The travellers came and went
proclaimed enemies of the same forgetfulness and the
    same passion
woodcutters always of the same longing
and stretching out before them as far as the eye and
    heart can reach
are the same ragged black clouds
tangling their masts
rusting their anchors
secretly wailing in their ears with the siren
that same sorrow

so to speak a bright yellow
gold
were colouring that black, that sad and wretched
    spot
cruelly pierced
by the drowsy lights of the electric lamps
the drowsy lights of a pitiable — ideal — prostitution
and the mangy camel's sleepy "che vuoi?"

so to speak?

consider that it's impossible
that it's completely pointless to blurt out and tell
of all this flame

ὅπου τρώει τά σωθικά σου
καί τήν κρατᾶς
ἔ, σύ!
τόσο καλά
τόσο σφιχτά
τόσο βαθειά φυλακισμένη
μέσα σου

οἱ ταξιδιῶτες λές ἐφύγαν ἤρθανε
ἐλύσανε τά μάγια
λύσανε τίς πριμάτσες
πού τούς κρατούσανε δεμένους στό μουράγιο
; δέν εἴταν
ἕνας χορός εὐγενικά θλιμμένος
ὅλες τοῦτες οἱ ἐξάρσεις τῶν νοσταλγῶν
πού σβεῖ τό κῦμα
ὡς δαγκάνει λυσσαγμένο
τῶν πεύκων τῶν ἀναμαλλιάρικων τό δίχτυ;
τῶν πεύκων πού ἐμεταμφιέστηκαν μόνο γι' ἀπόψε
μόνο
γιά νά γενοῦν κομῆτες;

ἕνα πουλί θαλασσινό τανύζει
τά φτερά του
λέει:
«ἐσύ 'σαι
ὁ νέος προφήτης
μέσα στήν τάφρο τῶν δικῶν σου λιονταριῶν»

eating away at your entrails
and you keep it
yes, you!
so well
so tightly
so deeply caged
inside you

the travellers so to speak then went and came
undid the spells
undid the cables
holding them bound to the quay
was it not
a nobly sorrowful dance
all that euphoria of the homesick
that the waves douse
when raging they champ
at the dishevelled pines' net?
pines disguised only for tonight
only
to beget comets?

a sea bird stretches
its wings
says:
"you are
the new prophet
in your own lions' pit"

Η ΚΥΡΙΑ ΟΥΡΑΝΙΑ

Ἐκείνη πού, φυσικά, ἐνυπάρχει στό χιονοσκέπαστο ἐνδιαίτημα τοῦ Βυζαντίου, δέν μπορεῖ νά παίζῃ στά ὑπαίθρια σκοπευτήριά μας μέ τίς δεισιδαιμονίες πολυπληθῶν ταγμάτων Δυτικῶν μοναχῶν. Ἡ προοπτική της εἶναι δυσάρεστη, ἡ πραγματογνωμοσύνη της κακή, τό σημεῖον αὐτό τῶν 6.500 μέτρων τοῦ ὕψους της ἔχει φανατικούς ὀπαδούς, κι' ὅμως, γιά νά ἀντιληφθῆ κανείς τό μέγεθος τοῦ χαμοῦ της δέν ἀρκεῖ ἡ μαρτυρία τῶν ἀπείρων παιδιῶν της, οἱ βεβαιώσεις τῶν ἀμέτρητων ἐραστῶν της, τό συμπέρασμα τῶν «κολχόζ» τῶν ἀνόμων πόθων της. Οἱ χειροπέδες τῆς Ἁγίας Σοφίας, ἡ ἐλπίδα τοῦ ἔθνους, τό «ποτό τῶν πεδιάδων», ἰδού στοιχεῖα λησμονιᾶς, φθόνου, ὀργῆς ὅσον καί συγγνώμης, ἰδού στοιχεῖα ὑπέρ αὐτῆς, πάντῃ λησμονημένα, τά ὁποῖα ἡμεῖς θέλουμε κι' ὑπενθυμίζουμε σέ μιάν ἀπεγνωσμένη οἱονεί προσπάθειαν ἐξιλέωσης ἅμα καί θαυμασμοῦ. Τό ὄνομά της, Εὐτέρπη. Μή μοῦ πῆτε τώρα ὅτι ποτέ δέν ἄξισε τά καυτερά δάκρυα πού ἐχύσαμε στήν ποδιά της, τόν λιβανωτό λατρείας καί πόθου πού ἐκαίαμε μπρός στήν εἰκόνα τῶν μαστῶν της, τήν ἀναμμένη λαμπάδα πού ἐστήναμε, ἑκάστοτε, στήν μνήμη τῶν πτερῶν μέ τά ὁποῖα κοσμοῦσε τά περίφημα, ἄλλωστε, καπέλλα της. Ὅθεν οἱ φαντασμοί τοῦ «ἄναρχου» δέν ἔχουν θέσιν ἐδῶ, τούτη τή στιγμή. Ἡ θερμοκρασία τῆς νύχτας δέν ἀποτολμᾶ τίποτε ἐναντίον τῶν θανασίμων παγίδων, τό ψάρεμα. Πατρίς δέ τῆς Δημοκρατίας, ἡ Κιβωτός καί τό ἐγκώμιον.

From: *In the flourishing Greek tongue*

LADY CELESTE

She who, naturally, is inherent in Byzantium's snow-covered abode, is unable to play in our outdoor shooting ranges with the superstitions of multitudinous orders of Western monks. Her perspective is unpleasant, her expertise poor, her spot with its altitude of 6,500 metres has fanatical adherents, and yet, to understand the magnitude of her loss requires more than the testimony of her infinite children, the assurances of her innumerable lovers, the conclusion of the "colchoz" of her illicit desires. The handcuffs of Haghia Sophia, the hope of the nation, the "drink of the plains", behold elements of forgetfulness, of envy, of anger and also of forgiveness, behold elements to her credit, forgotten by all, which we want to remind to all in an ostensibly desperate attempt at atonement and also admiration. Her name: Euterpe. Don't tell me now that she never deserved the burning tears we shed at her feet, the incense of worship and desire that we burned before the icon of her breasts, the burning candle we placed each time in memory of the wings with which she adorned her, in any case, renowned hats. Hence the fantasies of the "boundless" have no place here, at this time. The night's temperature risks nothing against the deadly snares, the fishing. Homeland of Democracy, the Ark and the encomium.

ΟΡΦΕΥΣ ΞΕΝΟΦΟΒΟΣ

τά δάκρυα λερώνουν τή ζωή

ἐκλάψατε τόσο πολύ
καί τώρα τά μάτια σας ἐστέρεψαν
γυναῖκες
τῆς Ἑλλάδας

ἐκεῖ πού ἐπέσαν τά ματόκλαδά σας
φυτρώνουν κυπαρίσσια
μέ πάντοτε στήν κορυφή τους
ἕνα πουλί

ORPHEUS XENOPHOBE

tears stain life

you wept so much
and now your eyes are run dry
women
of Greece

where your eyelashes fell
grow cypress trees
with always at their top
a bird

ΠΟΙΗΜΑ-ΑΠΟΜΙΜΗΣΙΣ ΠΟΛΛΩΝ ΨΑΛΜΩΝ ΑΡΜΟΣΜΕΝΟ ΓΙ' ΑΠΟΚΛΕΙΣΤΙΚΑ ΑΝΔΡΙΚΗ ΧΟΡΩΔΙΑ Σ' ΕΚΚΛΗΣΙΑΣΤΙΚΗ ΜΟΥΣΙΚΗ ΤΟΥ ΙΩΑΝΝΟΥ ΣΕΒΑΣΤΙΑΝΟΥ ΜΠΑΧ

κ α τ ά ρ α — Κύριε — σ' ὅποιον ἐπιβουλεύτηκε
τὸ ψωμὶ τοῦ ποιητοῦ
κατάρα — Κύριε — σ' ἐκεῖνον ὅπου ἔβαλε βέβηλο χέρι
στὰ λιγοστὰ χρήματα τοῦ
πτωχοῦ ζωγράφου
ποὔκλεψε τὴ δεκάρα
ἀπὸ τὴν τεταμένη
τὴν ταπεινὴ
τοῦ διακονιάρη
φούχτα
κ α τ ά ρ α !

χ α ρ ά μ ι !
φαρμάκι θὰ γένη τὸ ψωμί!
καὶ τὸ κλεμμένο νόμισμα:
καρφὶ πυραχτωμένο στ' ἄσπλαχνα τὰ στήθη
αὐτῶν ποὺ ἔστερξαν τὶς ἀνομίες
σ' αὐτοὺς π' ἀδίκησαν τὴ φτωχὴ χήρα
ποὺ ἔβαρέσαν τὸ ἀπροστάτευτο παιδὶ
ποὺ σπάσανε τὸ πήλινο τοῦ διψασμένου τάσι
π' ἀρνήθηκαν στὸν ἄρρωστο συμπόνια
ποὺ κοροϊδέψαν τὸ λεπρὸ
χτύπησαν τὸν τρελλὸ
καὶ τὸν τυφλὸ παραπλανῆσαν

From: *In the vale of roseries*

POEM-IMITATION OF NUMEROUS HYMNS SUITABLE FOR AN ALL-MALE CHOIR TO ECCLESIASTICAL MUSIC BY JOHANN SEBASTIAN BACH

a c c u r s e d — Lord — be whoever coveted
the poet's bread
accursed — Lord — be whoever lay an unholy hand
on the scant money of
the poor painter
who stole the penny
from the beggar's
humble
held-out
palm
a c c u r s e d!

t o n o a v a i l!
the bread will become poison!
and the stolen coin:
a red-hot spike in the cruel breast
of those who consented to the wicked acts
in those who wronged the poor widow
who beat the defenceless child
who broke the thirsting man's clay cup
who refused the sick compassion
who ridiculed the leper
struck the fool
and led the blind astray

ποὺ δυσκολέψαν τὴ ζωὴ τ' ἀνήμπορου
στοὺς ψεύδορκους
στοὺς ἀτιμάσαντες
σ' αὐτοὺς ποὺ βασανίσανε Ὁβραίους εἴτε Χριστιανοὺς
μέσ' στ' ἄνομα στρατόπεδα τῆς Γερμανίας

ὑ π ά ρ χ ε ι Θ ε ό ς !

ἡ μέρα περνᾶ
ἡ ὥρα περνᾶ
«ἡ κοινωνία γελᾶ»
σώζονται τὰ προσχήματα
ὅμως αὐτὸς δὲν τὸ κατάλαβε
ποὺ ἔπεσε νὰ κοιμηθῆ ἀφοῦ διέπραξε τὴν ἀνομία
πῶς ξημερώθηκε καὶ ξύπνησε καὶ περπατεῖ
πλέον μέσ' στὴ φοβερὴ μαυρίλα τοῦ θανάτου
(τὸ στόμα του ἀπὸ τώρα γέμισε χώματα)
κι' αὐτοῦ ποὺ ψεύστηκε
κι' αὐτοῦ π' ἀδίκησε
κι' αὐτοῦ ποὺ βάρεσε
θὰν τὸ πλερώσουνε καὶ τὰ παιδιά τους
καὶ λόγο — ὁπωσδήποτε — θὰ δώσουν
ἴσαμε καὶ
δεκάτη πέμπτη γενεὰ

ὑ π ά ρ χ ε ι Θ ε ό ς !

ἐτάζονται οἱ καρδιὲς καὶ τὰ νεφρά!
καὶ πλάϊ ἀπ' τὴ σακάτικη τὴ δικαιοσύνη τῶν ἀνθρώπω
κρύφτεται ἡ Ἐρινύα

who made life hard for the helpless
in the perjurers
in the violators
in those who tortured Jews or Christians
inside Germany's wicked camps

t h e r e ' s a G o d !

the day passes
the time passes
"society laughs"
excuses are at an end
yet the one who after committing the wicked act
went to sleep hasn't understood
that dawn has broken he's awake and walks
now in the dreadful gloom of death
(his mouth already filled with earth)
of the one to whom he lied
of the one he wronged
of the one he struck
their children will pay for it too
and will — undoubtedly — have to answer
down to
the fifteenth generation

t h e r e ' s a G o d !

hearts are vowed and kidneys!
and beside the crippled justice of humans
the Fury hides

βαθειὰ μέσα στὸν ἴδιο φταίχτη φωλιασμένη
ἀμείλιχτη ἀνελέητη
ποὺ καλὰ ροῦχα καὶ ὀφφίκια καὶ νομιμοφάνειες δὲν ψηφᾶ
ποὺ ἡ καλοπέραση — μὰ πρὸς Θεοῦ! — δὲν τηνὲ νοιάζει
καὶ τιμωρεῖ
σκληρὰ
τοὺς ἄμυαλους καὶ τοὺς δειλοὺς ποὺ κάνουν τὸ κακὸ
γιατὶ

ὑ π ά ρ χ ε ι   Θ ε ό ς !

ἔ! σὺ ἐπίορκε
— ναὶ σὺ ὅπου ψευδόρκησες —
ἐσὺ ποὺ ἔβλαψες μὲ τόσην ἀλαφριὰ — τὸν πλησίον σου
— συνείδηση
ἀπὸ τώρα ἀκοῦς στῆς νεκρικῆς σου ἀκολουθίας
τὰ ψαλσίματα
τοῦ πονηροῦ τοῦ πνεύματος τὰ γέλια
νὰ σαρκάζουν;
ἔ! ψεύτη ἀστὲ ὅσο κι' ἂν προσπαθεῖς
τὴ μούρη σου
γιὰ συμπαθητικὴ — κι' ὡραία ἀκόμη — νὰ μᾶς δείξης
μὴ χάνεσαι:
τὴ λούζει ἀλάκερη
τῆς ἔρημης ψυχῆς σου
ἡ βρώμα
κι' ἡ ἀνανδρία
κι' ἡ ψευτιὰ

ὑ π ά ρ χ ε ι   Θ ε ό ς !

nestled deep within the very culprit
merciless relentless
who heeds not fine clothes and titles and semblance
who — God forbid! — cares nothing for a pleasant life
and punishes
severely
the senseless and the cowards who do wrong
because

t h e r e ' s a G o d !

hey you! perjurer
— yes you who bore false witness —
you who — with such ease of conscience — harmed
    your neighbour
can you hear even now the chanting
of your funeral service
the laughter of the evil spirit
mocking you?
hey! bourgeois liar however much you try
to make your face
seem likeable — even nice — to us
you can't hide:
it's completely bathed
in the filth
of your desolate soul
in its cravenness
in its falsehood

t h e r e ' s a G o d !

ὅπως τοῦ δίκαιου τὸ κάθε τὶ θὲ νὰ γενῆ χαλάλι
ὁ ἀνομήσας — μὴ σᾶς νοιάζη — θὰ κριθῆ

ἀκούσατε τὰ λόγια αὐτὰ τοῦ ποιητῆ:
τὸ ἄνομο ψωμὶ δὲν ὠφελεῖ
ὑπάρχει ὁπωσδήποτε Θεός:

τί κρῖμα ὅμως νἄν' οἱ ἄνθρῶποι τόσο λίγοι!

just as all the righteous do will be rewarded
the wicked — don't worry — will be judged

hear these the poet's words:
illicit bread is of no benefit
there's definitely a God:

but what a shame that humans should be so few!

Η ΕΙΚΩΝ

τὰ σκυλιὰ π' ἀλυχτοῦν μέσα στὴ νύχτα
ὁ βαθὺς ἴσκιος τῶν δέντρων
τὸ πρωϊνὸ κελάδημα τοῦ κορυδαλλοῦ
τὸ τραγοῦδι τοῦ νεροῦ ποὺ τρέχει ἀπὸ τὴν πηγὴ
τί ἀνταμοιβὴ — ἡ μόνη —
γιὰ τὰ βαλαντώματα
τοὺς γόους
τὶς οἰμωγὲς
αὐτῶν ποὺ πρόλαβε ἡ καταιγίδα
αὐτῶν ποὺ τοὺς ἐβασάνισαν τὰ πονηρὰ δαιμόνια
αὐτῶν ποὺ αἰσθάνθηκαν
— ὀδυνηρὰ βέβαια —
ὅλες τὶς ἀποχρώσεις καὶ
τῶν αἰσθημάτων καὶ τῶν χρωμάτων
τὸ ρέκασμα τῆς ἀγωνίας
καὶ τ' ἁπαλὸ μινύρισμα τῆς τρυγόνας

ἂς ρίξουμε λουλούδια ἐκεῖ ποὺ ἐστάθηκε τὸ τέρας
ἂς ὁδηγήσουμε στὰ εὐεργετικὰ φρέατα τοὺς «ἀπολύτους
    ἐραστὰς τῆς ἀληθείας»

ἂς ὁρκισθοῦμε πὼς δὲν θὰ πεθάνουμε ποτὲ

THE ICON

the dogs that bark in the night
the trees' deep shade
the lark's morning trill
the song of the water running from the spring
what recompense — the only one —
for the languishing
the lamentations
the wailing
of those caught out by the storm
of those tormented by the evil demons
of those who felt
— painfully so of course —
all the shades both
of sentiments and colours
the wild cry of anguish
and the turtle-dove's soft cooing

let us cast flowers where the beast stood
let us lead "truth's consummate lovers" to the beneficent
    wells

let us vow that we will never die

ΤΩΝ ΙΕΡΩΝ ΕΒΡΑΙΩΝ...

εἰς μνήμην Ἀδόλφου Ἀβραὰμ Κάτζ

ὁ ραββῖνος τοῦ Γκέττο Νουόβο
εἶναι φίλος μου

αἰσθάνεται ἰδιαίτερη συμπάθεια γιὰ τὸ
κοκκινομάλλικο μικρὸ ἀγόρι
ποὺ εἴμουνα τότε
καθὼς μὲ βλέπει
τόσο θερμὰ προσηλωμένο
νὰ τὸν ἀκούω νὰ μοῦ μιλᾶ
γιὰ τ' ἄφταστα τὰ μεγαλεῖα τοῦ ἰουδαϊσμοῦ

καμμιὰ φορὰ — μὰ πολὺ σπάνια — σταματᾶ
ἡ ἐμπιστοσύνη του κλονίζεται
στέκει
μὲ κυττάζει
— στὸ κάτω-κάτω τῆς γραφῆς τί εἶμαι; ἕνας «γκόγι» —
συνέρχεται ὅμως σύντομα
καὶ συνεχίζει:
«ὑπάρχει ἄλλωστε — δικαιολογιέται — τοῦ Μεγ'-Ἀλέξαν-
δρου τὸ προηγούμενο»

ὁ νεωκόρος κατάγεται ἀπὸ τὴν Οὐκρανία
εἶναι κι' αὐτὸς «κοὲν»
(ὁ πατέρας του εἴτανε — τὸ λέει μ' ὑπερηφάνεια —
«τζελέπης»)
— προέρχεται κι' αὐτὸς ἀπὸ τὴν
οἰκογένεια τοῦ Λευΐ —

ON THE HOLY JEWS...

in memory of Adolf Abraham Katz

the rabbi in the Ghetto Nuovo
is a friend of mine

he is particularly fond of the
little redheaded boy
I was back then
seeing me
so deeply absorbed
in listening to him talking to me
about Judaism's unequalled splendour

occasionally — though very rarely — he stops
his confidence shaken
he stands
stares at me
— after all what am I? a "goy" —
but he soon recovers
and continues:
"and besides — justifying himself — there's the precedence with Alexander the Great"

the verger hails from the Ukraine
he too is a "Cohen"
(his father — he says with pride — was "well-to-do")
— he too comes from
the family of Levi —

ὅμως ἡ σταδιοδρομία του στὴν ἱεραρχία
τῆς Συναγωγῆς
προσέκρουσε σὲ κάτι οὐλὲς ποὺ ἔχει στὸ πρόσωπο
(προκοπὲς τῶν παιδικῶνε χρόνων)
 καὶ ὅπου δὲν τοῦ ἐπιτρέπουν
νὰ σταθῆ ἐνώπιον
τοῦ Αἰωνίου
τοῦ Τρισευλογημένου καὶ
Τρομεροῦ

ἡ κόρη τοῦ ραββίνου μὲ συναντᾶ
μόλις βραδυάσει
πλάϊ στὸ νερὸ
καὶ κάθε βράδυ μὲ χαμηλωμένα μάτια μὲ πληροφορεῖ
    πὼς μ' ἀγαπᾶ

ἡ γαϊτανοφρύδα Ὁβριοπούλα
ὡς φαίνεται δὲν θὰ μοῦ εἴτανε ἀδιάφορη:
στὰ μελλούμενα ποιήματά μου
θὰ ἐμφανίζεται ἐπίμονα
θὰ παρελαύνη
— πάντα γοητευτικὴ
καὶ μεγαλόπρεπη
κι' ὡραία —
βέβαια μὲ διαφορετικὰ ὀνόματα κάθε φορὰ
(ἄλλοτε ὡς
Λία
ἄλλοτε ὡς Ρεβέκκα
κι' ἄλλοτε πάλι ὡς
Ἐσθὴρ)

but his career in the hierarchy
of the Synagogue
came up against the scars he has on his face
(trophies from his childhood)
and which don't allow him
to stand before
the Eternal
the Thrice-blessed
and Terrible

the rabbi's daughter meets me
as soon as night falls
beside the water
and every night with eyes lowered she tells me that she
    loves me

this Hebrew girl with her fine eyebrows
clearly would not leave me indifferent:
in my future poems
she constantly appears
parades
— ever charming
and majestic
and lovely —
naturally with a different name each time
(sometimes as
Leah
sometimes as Rebecca
and again sometimes as
Esther)

Ο ΓΡΥΛΛΟΣ

εἰς Νάνον Βαλαωρίτην

τὸ μπαϊράκι — τὸ λάβαρο —
τῆς ζωῆς καὶ τῆς ἡμέρας
εἶν' πλουμισμένο
μὲ σωροὺς πολύχρωμες κορδέλλες
χάντρες
καὶ μὲ μακρυοὺς
κόκκινους θυσάνους

οἱ πολύχρωμες κορδέλλες
εἶναι οἱ χαρὲς
τὰ τραγούδια μας
τὰ ὄνειρά μας
μᾶς συνοδεύουνε στὶς ἔρημες ἀκρογιαλιὲς
εἶναι οἱ λατέρνες
ποὺ παίζουνε κάτ' ἀπ' τὰ δέντρα:
σὰ σουλατσάρουμε στὸ δάσος
μᾶς λένε τῆς βροχῆς τὶς ἑρμηνεῖες

τὰ μυστικὰ φωτίζονται
ἀπ' ἐκθαμβωτικὰ ἀστροπελέκια
τὰ πελέκια τσακίζουνε
τὶς κακὲς προθέσεις
κι' ὅλος ὁ κόσμος ἠχολογάει
ἀπὸ φωνὲς
παιδιῶν

THE CRICKET

to Nanos Valaoritis

the standard — the banner —
of life and day
is decked
with heaps of coloured ribbons
beads
and long
red tassels

the coloured ribbons
are our joys
our songs
our dreams
they accompany us on deserted shores
they are the barrel-organs
that play beneath the trees:
when we saunter in the wood
they give us interpretations of the rain

the secrets are illumined
by dazzling lightning bolts
the bolts shatter
evil intentions
and the whole world resounds
with voices
of children

σατύρων
καὶ τοῦ Ghirlandajo

οἱ χάντρες εἶναι τῶν καφφενείων οἱ καρέκλες
— τῶν καφφενείων ὅπ' ἀπαγορεύονται
οἱ παθιασμένες
τῆς πολιτικῆς
οἱ συζητήσεις ἢ τὸ τάβλι —

κι' ὅταν πλακώσουνε οἱ βαρειές μας
οἱ σκοτοῦρες
τότες μπαίνουνε οἱ θύσανοι σ' ἐνέργεια
οἱ μπελιάδες σκορποῦνε
μακρυά μας
σὰν ἀπὸ θαῦμα
τὰ σύννεφα διαλύονται
λάμπει ὁ ἥλιος πάλε
τὰ δάκρυα στερεύουν
παύουν οἱ σειρῆνες
κι' ἐλεύθεροι
σκαμπανεβάζουμε
στοῦ
ἔρωτα
τὶς μαοῦνες καὶ τὶς βάρκες

στὶς συνοικίες τῆς πόλεως βαροῦνε οἱ καμπάνες
στῆς Τρούμπας τὰ σοκάκια
χαλοῦν τὸν κόσμο
οἱ κιθάρες
ὅπως στοὺς μύλους (τοὺς μύθους)

of satyrs
and of Ghirlandajo

the beads are chairs in cafés
— cafés which prohibit
passionate
political
discussions and backgammon —

and when we're beset by weighty
concerns
it's then that the tassels come into play
the troubles scatter
far from us
as if by miracle
the clouds dissolve
the sun shines again
the tears dry up
the sirens cease
and free
we're tossed
on
love's
barges and boats

in the city's districts the bells peal
in Troumba's backstreets
guitars
cause a stir
as in mills (myths)

μᾶς ἀλέθουν
τὰ τολμήματα
τῶν σαυροκτόνων

κι' ἔρχετ' ἡ δύση
ἡ Δύση
κι' ὅλα πᾶν χαημένα

they grind for us
the feats
of dragon-slayers

then the sun sinks in the west
the West
and everything is wasted

ΠΕΡΙ ΑΜΑΔΡΥΑΔΩΝ

τὴ λεύκα ποὺ ἀντικρύζω
ἀπὸ τὸ παρεθύρι μου
τὴν ἀγαπῶ

χρόνια τώρα — χειμῶνα καλοκαῖρι — τὴν παρακολουθῶ
ἀπὸ τοῦ σύνεγγυς
ἄλλοτε μὲ τὶς φουντωτὲς τὶς φυλλωσιὲς
ἄλλοτε μὲ τὰ ξερά της τὰ κλαριὰ
μέσ' στοὺς βοριάδες

ὅμως ποτέ μου δὲν τὴν εἶδα τὴν ἁμαδρυάδα
της
ποὺ πρέπει νὰ τὴν κατοικῆ
ὅσο καὶ ἂν ἐπρόσεξα
ὅσο κι' ἂν ὧρες ἀτέλειωτες
δὲν ἔπαψα κρυφὰ
νὰ τηνὲ παρακολουθῶ

: ἴσως νὰ μὴν ὑπῆρξαν οἱ ἁμαδρυάδες;
αὐτὸ ὅμως
δὲν τὄπε ποτὲ κανείς!

λέω μήπως ἀπόθανε ἀπὸ καιρὸ
ἡ δικιά μου ἡ ἁμαδρυάδα
καὶ μήπως — ἀπὸ χρόνια τώρα —
νὰ προσετέθηκε κι' αὐτὴ
στὶς τόσο ἀμείλικτες
καὶ τόσο ἀφόρητα βασανιστικὲς γύρω μας
ἀπουσίες;

CONCERNING HAMADRYADS

the poplar I look onto
from my window
is one I dearly love

for years — in summer and winter — I've observed it
from close up
sometimes with its bushy leafage
sometimes with its bare branches
in the north winds

yet I never once saw
its hamadryad
that must dwell in it
however much I looked
however many hours
I spent secretly
observing it

perhaps hamadryads didn't exist?
yet such a thing
no one has ever said!

did my hamadryad I wonder
die long ago
and has she too been added
— these many years now —
to those so merciless
and so unbearably painful
absences?

ΤΟ ΠΟΙΗΜΑ ΤΗΣ ΕΣΘΗΡ ΜΠΕΣΣΑΛΕΛ

— *Καὶ ἡ Ἐστέρ;*
— *Τώρα ἔρχεται... ἡ δύστυχη...*
ALBERTO SAVINIO Ὁ Λορέντζος Μαβίλης

σὰν ξαναεπιστρέψω
στὴ Θεσσαλονίκη
ἀπὸ τὴν κόλαση
δὲν θὲ ν' ἀφήσω τοὺς ἀγαπητούς μου
τοὺς Ὀβραίους πάλι νὰ μὲ ζουρλάνουνε
μὲ τὰ
«:εἶδες Σολομωνίκο — τάδε σύνταγμα —
εἶδες Μωϋσῆ — στὸν τάδε λόχο
τάδε διμοιρία — ἢ
ἴσως νὰ ἐσυνάντησες τὸν Ἀβραμίκο πουθενά;...»
καὶ ἄλλα...

θὰ τοὺς ἁρπάξω ἀπ' τὰ μοῦτρα
τοὺς ἀγαθοὺς τοὺς πονεμένους ἀνθρώπους
καὶ μὲ φωνὲς καὶ μὲ σκουξίματα
θὰ ἐπιμείνω νὰ μοῦ ποῦν
ἂν συναντῆσαν πουθενὰ
ποτὲ
— καὶ τώρα ποῦ νὰ βρίσκεται; —
τὴν Ἐστερίκα
τὴ Ρίκα
τ' ἀστέρι τὸ λαμπρὸ
στὰ πρῶτα ἐρωτικά μου χρόνια τὰ νεανικὰ
τὰ μικράτα μου!

THE POEM OF ESTHER BESSALEL

> — *And Esther?*
> — *She's coming now... poor thing...*
> ALBERTO SAVINIO *Lorenzos Mavilis*

when again I return
to Salonica
from hell
I won't let my dear
Jews drive me mad once more
with their
"did you see young Solomon — such-and-such regiment —
did you see Moses — such-and-such company
such-and-such platoon — or
perhaps you ran into our Abraham somewhere?..."
and the like…

I'll grab them by the jowls
those simple those suffering people
and shouting and screaming
I'll insist that they tell me
if they've seen anywhere
ever
— and where might she be now? —
little Esther
Rika
the bright star
in the first amorous years of my youth
of my infancy!

ὤ! τὸ κελεποῦρι τοῦ μεγάλου παρισινοῦ βιβλιοπωλείου!
ἡ χαριτωμένη γαλλιδούλα!
(μὲ βαθειὲς ρίζες — ὅμως —
εἰς γῆν Χαναὰν)
ὤ! ἡ ὑπέροχη μαγνόλια!
ἡ κατάλευκη γαρδένια
τ' ἄσπρο μου γιασεμὶ
μὲ τὰ μαῦρα βελούδινα
σπανιόλικά της
μάτια

ὤ! ὁ ποιητικὸς ἀπόηχος
τῶν γιοφυριῶν πάνω στὸ Σηκουάνα
ἡ φουντωτὴ ἀνθισμένη καστανιὰ
τῶν μακρυῶν λεωφόρων
ἡ μαγευτικὴ γλυσίνα
τῶν ἀνακτορικῶν πάρκων
ἡ ἄκρως δονούμενη
θεσπέσια ἄρπα τοῦ Δαυΐδ!

μὰ πῶς τὴν ἔχασα
τὴν ἄφατη τὴν
εὐτυχία
ἀπ' τὰ χέρια μου!
οἱ δίνες τῆς ζωῆς ὑπῆρξαν ἡ αἰτία...

παντοῦ καὶ πάντα τὴν ἀναπολῶ
πάντα τῆ σκέφτομαι
κι' ὁ νοῦς μου τώρα καὶ πάντα εἶναι
κοντά της

O! the treasure of the huge Paris bookshop!
the pretty little French girl!
(with deep roots — however —
in the land of Canaan)
O! the wonderful magnolia!
the shining gardenia
my white jasmine
with her velvety black
Spanish
eyes

O! the poetic echo
of bridges over the Seine
the thick blossoming chestnut
of the long boulevards
the enchanting wisteria
of the imperial parks
the utterly vibrant
divine harp of David!

yet how did I lose
that indescribable
happiness
from out of my hands!
the maelstroms of life were the cause…

everywhere and always I recall her
always think of her
and now and always my mind is
with her

·μήπως νὰ μετανάστεψε — ὡς ποθοῦσε —
στὸ
«Ἐρὲτζ Ἰσραέλ»;
·μήπως μοῦ τὴν ἐκάμαν
λουλουδάκι
οἱ ἀπαίσιοι Νατσῆδες;
·ἢ μήπως τώρα νἄναι κάπου νὰ μαραίνεται
καὶ νὰ μὴ
μὲ θυμᾶται;

perhaps she emigrated — as was her wish —
to
"Eretz Israel"?
perhaps those horrid Nazis
made a tiny flower
of her?
or perhaps now she's withering somewhere
and doesn't
remember me?

ΤΟ ΞΑΦΝΙΑΣΜΑ

ἡ ἀγάπη
σὰν τὴ ζωὴ
εἶναι ἕνα ὄνειρο

μιὰ φούχτα ἄμμο
ὅσο σφιχτὰ — γερὰ — κι' ἂν τὴν κρατᾶς
σοῦ ξεγλυστρᾶ ἀπὸ τὰ δάχτυλα
ξεφεύγει καὶ πέφτει
κατὰ γῆς

τὸ μόνο σταθερό:
τὸ ὑπέροχο
τὸ θαυμαστὸ
τὸ φευγαλέο ὅραμα
τοῦ ρόδινου δικτυωτοῦ
καὶ τὰ ὁλόμαυρα μαλλάκια

;τὸ αἷμα;

THE SURPRISE

love
like life
is a dream

a handful of sand
however tightly — strongly — you clasp it
slips through your fingers
escapes and falls
to the ground

the one thing constant:
the wonderful
the marvellous
the fleeting vision
of the rosy network
with the jet black hair

the blood?

Self-portrait (1933)

Chronology

1907 (21 October): Born in Athens, second son of Panayotis and Errietti.

1914 (Summer): Family moves to Constantinople following the outbreak of the War.

1923-1927: Enrolled as a boarder in a lycée in Paris.

1927 (November) - 1928 (July): On returning to Athens, he undertakes his military service as a private in the 1st Infantry Regiment.

1928-1930: Works as a translator in a Bank and as a secretary at the University and attends night-school in order to obtain the Greek School-Leaving Certificate.

1930 (October) - 1933 (March): Employed on a daily basis as a designer in the Urban Planning Department of the Ministry of Public Works.

1932: Enrolls in the Athens School of Fine Arts where he studies under Konstantinos Parthenis. He also studies at the studio of Fotis Kontoglou.

1934 (May): Appointed as an employee in the Topographical Service at the Ministry of Public Works and is given tenure exactly six years later.

1937: Father dies in Constantinople.

1938 (January): First presentation of his works (temperas on paper depicting old houses from towns in Western

Macedonia) at the exhibition "Art of the Modern Greek Tradition". (February): Translates poems by Tristan Tzara and publishes them in the volume *Sur(r)ealism I*. Finishes his studies (receiving his diploma in January 1956). (June): Publishes his first collection of poetry: *Do Not Distract the Driver* (Athens: Kyklos) and designs the sets and costumes for Plautus' *Menaechmi* (directed by Yannoulis Sarandidis at the Kotopouli Theatre).

1939 (September): Publication of his second collection: *The Clavicembalos of Silence* (Athens: Hippalektryon). (November): First individual exhibition at the home of Nikos Kalamaris. Designs the sets and costumes for Sophocles' *Electra* (directed by Karolos Koun at the Kotopouli Theatre). Participates in a group exhibition of Greek artists in New York.

1941 (January): Called up to the Albanian Front.

1942: Participates in the "Professional" Painting Exhibition at the Zappeion Megaron, and again in the following year. Writes *Bolivar, a Greek Poem*. The poem initially circulated in manuscript form and was read at gatherings expressing resistance to the Nazi Occupation.

1944 (September): Publication of *Bolivar, a Greek Poem* (Athens: Ikaros).

1945 (May): Seconded from the Ministry of Public Works to the National Technical University of Athens as an assistant lecturer in the Department of Architectural Design and Drawing and remains in this post with continual renewals of the secondment until 1956. Designs the sets and costumes for Nikos Kazantzakis' play *Capodistria* (directed by Socrates Karantinos at the National Theatre).

1946 (May): Publication of his collection, *The Return of the Birds* (Athens: Ikaros).

1948 (December): Publication of his collection, *Eleusis* (Athens: Ikaros).

1949: Participates in the Pan-Hellenic Exhibition at the Zappeion Megaron (and again in 1952, 1957, 1963, 1965, 1971, 1973 and 1975). Becomes a founding member of the art group "Armos", which has as its aim to promote a modern aesthetic movement in Greece. Exhibits works with the "Armos" group in the same year and again in 1950 (Athens and Thessaloniki) and in 1952. His paintings are also exhibited at the Greek pavilion in the International Exhibition in New York.

1950 (March): Marriage to Nelly Andrikopoulou.

1951: Participates in a group exhibition of Stage Scenery in Oslo, in those organised by the International Theatre Institute in Athens in 1957 and 1962, and in the one organised by the French Institute of Athens in December 1959. Also participates in the exhibition organised by the International Association of Architects in Athens (and again in 1954). Birth of his son Panos.

1952: Designs the scenery and costumes for Goldoni's *Il burbero di buon cuore* (directed by Socrates Karantinos at the National Theatre). Assists in the painting of the frescoes in the church of St Spyridon in New York (undertaken by Fotis Kontoglou).

1953: Participates in a group exhibition of Greek painters in Rome and Ottawa (and later in Edmonton, Toronto and Vancouver in 1954 and São Paulo in 1955).

1954: Publishes his long poem, "The Atlantic", in the magazine *Anglo-Elliniki Epitheorisi* (Vol. 6, no. 3) together with an oil-painting (Jason). (Summer): Represents Greece in the 27th International Biennale in Venice with 72 of his works. Divorced from his wife, Nelly Andrikopoulou.

1956 (June): Elected to the National Technical University of Athens as a tenured lecturer and appointed to the Department of Architectural Design and Drawing. Resigns from the Ministry of Public Works.

1957 (April): Publication of his collection, *In the Flourishing Greek Tongue* (Athens: Ikaros). (May): Appointed as a lecturer in the Department of General Art History. Participates in a group exhibition of painting in Thessaloniki (and again in 1966 and 1973). Designs the scenery and costumes for *Girl, Aspects of a Woman, Medea* and *Ring and Trumpet* for Rallou Manou's "Greek Ballet".

1958 (December): Awarded the First Prize for Poetry by the Ministry of National Education for his collection, *In the Flourishing Greek Tongue*.

1959: Participates in the group exhibition organized by "Zygos". Designs the scenery and costumes for Euripides' *Ion* and Aeschylus' *Prometheus Bound* (directed by Linos Karzis for the "Themelikos Theatre Company").

1960: Second marriage to Eleni Tsiokou. (May): Appointed as supervisor to the Modelling Studio. (August): Journey to Switzerland, Germany and Austria.

1961: Birth of his daughter Errietti.

1962 (June): Designs the scenery and costumes for Brecht's *The Threepenny Opera* (directed by Nikos Hatziskos), for Shaw's *Caesar and Cleopatra* (directed by Alexis Solomos) and for Molière's *Le Bourgeois Gentilhomme* (directed by Socrates Karantinos for the State Theatre of Northern Greece). (December): Second edition of *Bolivar, a Greek Poem* with notes and 8 colour plates (Athens: Ikaros).

1963 (February): Individual exhibition of painting at the Athens Technological Institute. Mother dies in Athens.

1964 (January): Participates in the Commemorative Exhibition for Yorgos Bouzianis and Dimitris K. Evanghelidis. (February): Resigns from the National Technical University. Designs the scenery and costumes for Euripides' *Hippolytus* (directed by Socrates Karantinos for the State Theatre of Northern Greece). Participates in a group exhibition of Greek painters in Brussels. (November): Release of the record *Engonopoulos Reads Engonopoulos* on the "Dionysos" label.

1965: Designs the scenery and costumes for Aristophanes' *Lysistrata* (directed by Socrates Karantinos for the State Theatre of Northern Greece).

1966 (May): Awarded the Order of the Gold Cross of George I for his work as a painter. (October): Second edition of *Do Not Distract the Driver* and *The Clavicembalos of Silence* in one volume with notes and an autobiographical note (Athens: Ikaros).

1967 (October): Elected non-tenured Professor at the National Technical University in the Department of Drawing.

1968 (December): Release of the record *Bolivar, a Greek Poem* on the Lyra label, as a popular cantata, with music by Nikos Mamangakis and vocals by Yorgos Zografos.

1969 (April): Elected tenured Professor at the National Technical University in the Department of Drawing and authorized Professor in the Department of General Art History.

1971: Participates in the exhibition "Modern Greek Art on the 1821 War of Independence. Painting - Sculpture - Engraving" at the Greek Chamber of Art. (December): Awarded the Cross of the Commander of the Phoenix.

1972: Publication by the National Technical University of Athens Press of the album *Hellenic Houses*, containing 18 colour paintings.

1973 (August): Retires from the National Technical University (becoming Professor Emeritus in 1976).

1976 (November): Exhibition of his paintings at the Moraitis School's Society for the Study of Modern Greek Culture and General Education.

1977 (November): Publication of the second volume of his *Poems*, containing the collections: *Bolivar, The Return of the Birds, Eleusis, The Atlantic* and *In the Flourishing Greek Tongue* (Athens: Ikaros).

1978 (November): Publication of his collection, *In the Vale of Roseries,* with 20 colour plates and one sketch (Athens: Ikaros).

1979: Awarded the National Prize for Poetry for the second time.

1980 (November): Publication of his study, *Karaghiozis. Greek Shadow Theatre* (Athens: Ypsilon/Books).

1983 (March): Retrospective exhibition of his work with 105 paintings at the National Gallery / Alexandros Soutsos Museum.

1984 (November): Individual exhibition of water-colours, sketches and temperas in the "Zoumboulaki" Art Gallery.

1985 (31 October): Dies of a heart attack. He is buried in the First Cemetery of Athens at public expense.

Adapted and translated from the biographical data provided on Engonopoulos's website (www.engonopoulos.gr) and compiled by I.M. Vourtsis.

Book-length English Translations

Ωραίος σαν Έλληνας. Ποιήματα / The Beauty of a Greek. Poems, Selected and Translated by David Connolly, Ypsilon Books: Athens, 2007.

Acropolis and Tram. Poems 1938-1978. Edited and Translated by Martin McKinsey, Green Integer: København & Los Angeles, 2008.

The Collected Works of Nikos Engonopoulos. Translated by Philip Ramp. Introduction by Yiorgis Yatromanolakis. Pygmy Forest Press: Springfield, OR, 2011.

Selected Poems. Translated with an Introduction and Notes by David Connolly, Harvard University Press: Cambridge MA, 2016.

Index of Greek Titles

Ἀμαζόνες 24
Ἀλεξιβρόχια 32
Ἄπατρις ἀπελαυνόμενος βίαια 84
Ἕνας αὐλός μέσ' στήν αὐλή τῆς ἑκατόμβης 30
«Ἐνθύμιον τῆς Κωνσταντινουπόλεως» 80
Ἡ εἰκών 104
Ἡ ἐρωτική πλεκτάνη 70
Ἡ κυρία Οὐρανία 92
Ἡ τελευταία ἐμφάνισις Ἰούδα τοῦ Ἰσκαριώτη 78
Ἴσως 26
Καφφενεῖα καί κομῆτες ὕστερα ἀπό τά μεσάνυχτα 88
Ὁ γρύλλος 110
Ὀρφεύς ξενόφοβος 94
Περί ἁμαδρυάδων 116
Ποίημα-ἀπομίμησις πολλῶν ψαλμῶν 96
Πολυξένη 22
Πρωϊνό τραγούδι 54
Στά ὄρη τῆς Μυουπόλεως 38
Συνέπεια 48
Τά ξοανόμορφα εἴδωλα τοῦ ἀερολιμένος 28
Τό ἔβδομο τραγούδι τῆς ἀγάπης 74
Τό ξάφνιασμα 124
Τό ποίημα τῆς Ἐσθήρ Μπεσσαλέλ 118
Τό τραγούδι ἑνοῦ στρατιώτη 60
Τῶν ἱερῶν Ἑβραίων 106

MODERN
GREEK
CLASSICS

C.P. CAVAFY
Selected Poems BILINGUAL EDITION
Translated by David Connolly

Cavafy is by far the most translated and well-known Greek poet internationally. Whether his subject matter is historical, philosophical or sensual, Cavafy's unique poetic voice is always recognizable by its ironical, suave, witty and world-weary tones.

ODYSSEUS ELYTIS
1979 NOBEL PRIZE FOR LITERATURE
In the Name of Luminosity and Transparency
With an Introduction by Dimitris Daskalopoulos

The poetry of Odysseus Elytis owes as much to the ancients and Byzantium as to the surrealists of the 1930s and the architecture of the Cyclades, bringing romantic modernism and structural experimentation to Greece. Collected here are the two speeches Elytis gave on his acceptance of the 1979 Nobel Prize for Literature.

M. KARAGATSIS
The Great Chimera
Translated by Patricia Barbeito

A psychological portrait of a young French woman, Marina, who marries a sailor and moves to the island of Syros, where she lives with her mother-in-law and becomes acquainted with the Greek way of life. Her fate grows entwined with that of the boats and when economic downturn arrives, it brings passion, life and death in its wake.

ANDREAS LASKARATOS
Reflections   BILINGUAL EDITION
Translated by Simon Darragh
With an Introduction by Yorgos Y. Alisandratos

Andreas Laskaratos was a writer and poet, a social thinker and, in many ways, a controversialist. His *Reflections* sets out, in a series of calm, clear and pithy aphorisms, his uncompromising and finely reasoned beliefs on morality, justice, personal conduct, power, tradition, religion and government.

ALEXANDROS PAPADIAMANDIS
Fey Folk
Translated by David Connolly

Alexandros Papadiamandis holds a special place in the history of Modern Greek letters, but also in the heart of the ordinary reader. *Fey Folk* follows the humble lives of quaint, simple-hearted folk living in accordance with centuries-old traditions and customs, described here with both reverence and humour.

ALEXANDROS RANGAVIS
The Notary
Translated by Simon Darragh

A mystery set on the island of Cephalonia on the eve of the Greek Revolution of 1821, this classic work of Rangavis is an iconic tale of suspense and intrigue, love and murder. *The Notary* is Modern Greek literature's contribution to the tradition of early crime fiction, alongside E.T.A. Hoffman, Edgar Allan Poe and Wilkie Collins.

EMMANUEL ROÏDES
Pope Joan
Translated by David Connolly

Roïdes' irreverent, witty and delightful novel tells the story of Joan who, according to a popular medieval legend, ascended to the Papal Throne as Pope John VIII. In Joan, Roïdes has created one of the most remarkable characters in modern Greek literature and in so doing has assured his place as one of its classic authors.

ANTONIS SAMARAKIS
The Flaw
Translated by Simon Darragh

A man is seized from his afternoon drink at the Cafe Sport by two agents of the Regime by car toward Special Branch Headquarters, and the interrogation that undoubtedly awaits him there. Part thriller and part political satire, *The Flaw* has been translated into more than thirty languages.

GEORGE SEFERIS
1963 NOBEL PRIZE FOR LITERATURE
Novel and Other Poems   BILINGUAL EDITION
Translated by Roderick Beaton

Often compared during his lifetime to T.S. Eliot, George Seferis is noted for his spare, laconic, dense and allusive verse in the Modernist idiom of the first half of the twentieth century. Seferis better than any other writer expresses the dilemma experienced by his countrymen then and now: how to be at once Greek and modern.

MAKIS TSITAS
God Is My Witness
Translated by Joshua Barley

A hilariously funny and achingly sad portrait of Greek society during the crisis years, as told by a lovable anti-hero. Fifty-year-old Chrysovalantis, who has recently lost his job and struggles with declining health, sets out to tell the story of his life, roaming the streets of Athens on Christmas Eve with nothing but a suitcase in hand.

ILIAS VENEZIS
Serenity
Translated by Joshua Barley

Inspired by the author's own experience of migration, the novel follows the journey of a group of Greek refugees from Asia Minor who settle in a village near Athens. It details the hatred of war, the love of nature that surrounds them, the hostility of their new neighbours and eventually their adaptation to a new life.

GEORGIOS VIZYENOS
Thracian Tales
Translated by Peter Mackridge

These short stories bring to life Vizyenos' native Thrace, a corner of Europe where Greece, Turkey and Bulgaria meet. Through masterful psychological portayals, each story keeps the reader in suspense to the very end: Where did Yorgis' grandfather travel on his only journey? What was Yorgis' mother's sin? Who was responsible for his brother's murder?

GEORGIOS VIZYENOS
Moskov Selim
Translated by Peter Mackridge

A novella by Georgios Vizyenos, one of Greece's best-loved writers, set in Thrace during the time of the Russo-Turkish War, whose outcome would decide the future of south-eastern Europe. *Moskov Selim* is a moving tale of kinship, despite the gulf of nationality and religion.

NIKIFOROS VRETTAKOS
Selected Poems
BILINGUAL EDITION

Translated by David Connolly

The poems of Vrettakos are firmly rooted in the Greek landscape and coloured by the Greek light, yet their themes and sentiment are ecumenical. His poetry offers a vision of the paradise that the world could be, but it is also imbued with a deep and painful awareness of the dark abyss that the world threatens to become.

AN ANTHOLOGY

Rebetika: Songs from the Old Greek Underworld

BILINGUAL EDITION

Edited and translated by Katharine Butterworth & Sara Schneider

The songs in this book are a sampling of the urban folk songs of Greece during the first half of the twentieth century. Often compared to American blues, rebetika songs are the creative expression of the *rebetes*, people living a marginal and often underworld existence on the fringes of established society.